796.5 EGG
Eggert, Richard.
Fish and hunt the backcountry
WASH. PUB. LIB

3 6910 99004901 5

Eggert, Richard
    Fish and hunt the backcountry.

stacks   796.5
                                          Egg

Date Due

APR 2 8 1982		
DEC 2 1 1982		
SEP 0 6 1983		
MAY 2 8 1985		
MAY 0 2 1995		

BRODART, INC.   Cat. No. 23 233

D1301100

FISH AND HUNT THE BACKCOUNTRY

BY RICHARD EGGERT

Stackpole Books

FISH AND HUNT THE BACKCOUNTRY

Copyright © 1978 by
Richard Eggert

Published by
STACKPOLE BOOKS
Cameron and Kelker Streets
P.O. Box 1831
Harrisburg, Pa. 17105

Published simultaneously in Don Mills, Ontario, Canada by Thomas
Nelson & Sons, Ltd.

All rights reserved, including the right to reproduce this book or portions thereof
in any form or by any means, electronic or mechanical, including photocopying,
recording, or by any information storage and retrieval system, without permis-
sion in writing from the publisher. All inquiries should be addressed to Stackpole
Books, Cameron and Kelker Streets, P.O. Box 1831, Harrisburg, Pennsylvania
17105.

Printed in the U.S.A.

Library of Congress Cataloging in Publication Data

Eggert, Richard.
    Fish and hunt the backcountry.

    Includes index.
    1. Hunting. 2. Fishing. 3. Wilderness survival.
I. Title.
SK33.E34   796.5   78-17135
ISBN 0-8117-0191-3

CONTENTS

4/9/82 *95 Outdoor Life Bk.

Introduction

It is a bright, brittle, sharply shimmering January day in western Montana's Mission Mountains. The peaks of the range outside my cabin window are like giant chips from mammoth ice cubes, starkly angular and glittering.

Fine winter days here almost always mean numbing cold, and the frozen air is crackling at well below zero.

The snow is stacked to the windowsill in front of my typewriter and I peer over the brim of a drift to see the crystal world outside. My car won't start—hasn't for a week—but that is all right because it couldn't go anywhere if it did. The gravel country roads on the valley floor are definable only by their proximity to rows of gray fencepost tops that peak timidly above the all-obscuring snow.

Getting out and about here in January is often a matter of foregoing modern modes of transportation and hoofing it on skis or snowshoes. Almost everybody here has a pair of one or both and using them can be a matter of primitive necessity, not just a way of enjoying ourselves.

People in this neck of the woods are inclined to pursue their sport in equally atavistic ways. Of course there are the four-wheelers, trailbikers, and snowmobilers here as elsewhere. These machines and the people who drive them are a product of our energy-wasteful times.

But most people here who like to hunt, fish, or poke around in nature have found an affinity between the backcountry and their muscles. They have found that getting off the roads and trails back into the marrow of the land has a way of sharpening their perception of the world and their quarry.

That is what this book is about: the backcountry—how to find it, travel in it, appreciate it, and expand your territory as a hunter, fisherman, or nature lover.

The land itself, this mysterious and arcane place we call back-country, is both the hub of all these activities and the common denominator of everything we will be talking about. Some kind of working definition of backcountry is therefore necessary.

In a way it could be said that this winter mountain world beyond my window is backcountry. In this place at this time there are few visible benchmarks of civilization. If I ski up the road a half mile to a little rise I can see houses protruding from the snow with thin wisps of friendly smoke trickling up through the brittle air. If I ski a mile or so farther I will cross paths with a federal highway and a few motorists. Telephone lines and utility poles remind me of the domesticated nature of my home.

However, in a purely functional sense I must travel by foot and am at the mercy of the elements. I can't drive my car, catch a bus, call a cab, hop in an elevator, or ride an escalator to see these monuments to mankind; I have to use my legs.

Does this mean I am writing these words from the fringe of the backcountry? Let's take a look.

The first place to look for a formal definition of our troublesome element is the dictionary. But none of the three dignified and usually reliable volumes I use acknowledge the word. No help there.

How about governmental agencies? They have at least a policy and usually a department for just about everything; maybe there is a Bureau of Backcountry or a code of backcountry regulations. However, the only local, state, or federal agency that gives backcountry a formal meaning is the U.S. Park Service, although most land management agencies do use the designation in a more general form.

Backcountry in Montana's Glacier National Park is several thousand acres of wild lands set aside and isolated from other aspects of the park's management. Only a few hikers are allowed into them at any time, animals and plants are left to their own devices, and natural forces, such as fires, are allowed to go about their work unimpeded.

Glacier's definition of backcountry starts with natural animal and plant communities and manages them only as much as necessary to maintain this critical ecological balance.

However, this book is not about one limited area in western Montana; it is designed to be useful anywhere there are wild lands. So we are going to have to expand our definition of backcountry.

Other federal agencies, such as the Forest Service and the Bureau of Land Management, use the word backcountry, only in a more vague sense. They use it to describe lands that have not been developed or have recovered from economic activity such as forestry but are not qualified for consideration as wilderness. Wilderness, as defined in the 1964 Wilderness Act is: "hereby recognized as an area where the earth and its community of life are untrammeled by man, where man himself is a visitor who does not remain . . . without permanent improvements or human habitation . . . which generally appears to have been affected primarily by forces of nature . . . has outstanding opportunities for solitude . . . has at least five thousand acres of land . . . and may also contain ecological, geological and other features of scientific, educational, scenic, or historical value."

Backcountry, to the Forest Service, is land not currently under commercial management but not qualified or desirable for Wilderness Act protection. The designation represents a state of limbo between development and a congressional commitment to the continuity of the wild character of the land.

There are currently some 12.3 million acres of statutory wilderness in the United States spread over 125 wilderness areas throughout the contiguous states. There are also 26.1 million acres being considered for wilderness classification on 112 proposed sites. In addition the U.S. Forest Service has some 187 million acres of land and there are another 631 million under state and private ownership. Although there is no precise quantification of backcountry forest lands, much of the national forest and a lot of state and private lands remain in primitive status.

So let's step back and see how our definition of backcountry is coming. So far it is more substance than form. Although we don't know exactly what it is, we do know there is a lot of it. We know that of the gross inventory of undeveloped federal and private lands some wilderness will retain its primitive integrity but most, we can be assured, will be changing in character through economic development.

Before we firm up our backcountry definition let's examine how this ample quantity of wild backcountry came to be—or, more accurately, how it avoided becoming something else. With rare exception, all backcountry—even parks and wilderness areas—remains wild only because something about it stood in the way of exploitation. It either didn't have what was regarded as sufficiently valuable natural resources or the character of its terrain—too high, too low, too wet, too dry—resisted attempts to extract resources.

For the most part, the remaining backcountry areas are rugged enough to repel the bulldozer and consequently a challenge to the footloose backcountry traveler. Like boulders in a river, these areas have been able to resist the mainstream current and they can still be found protruding above the flow of civilization just about everywhere in the United States.

This rugged, formidable quality of the backcountry we are talking about makes it a natural sanctuary for wild animals, birds, and fish. The habitat of these creatures has not been disturbed by machines and has escaped massive intrusion by convenience-oriented sportsmen. The land areas of our backcountry are large enough so the day-traveling hunter or fisherman cannot reach their remote heart, which is open only to those who are willing to overcome the distance and the terrain with their nomad home on their back.

Our definition of backcountry is now taking some meaningful form. Although it is more a quality than a quantity, it does have some palpable physical characteristics. It exists almost everywhere in the United States and Canada—sometimes as the predominant character of the land, sometimes as a wild island in a sea of civilization. It must be large enough and/or rugged enough to require at least a couple of days on foot to travel through it and remote enough to offer solace and solitude not only to its wild inhabitants but also to jaded travelers. It must have enough elbow room to isolate the traveler from the securities, pacifiers, and anxieties of civilization so that he has to rely on his skill, strength, and the meager equipment he can pack on his back.

Our backcountry, like the congressional definition of wilderness, must have enough contiguous wild lands to allow a population of game animals such as deer to exist in innocence. It must be isolated enough that timid waterfowl and upland birds can satisfy habitat requirements without constantly being exposed to the hot breath of lead shot. There must be lakes far enough from the reach of road and trail so that fish are unsophisticated in the devices of anglers.

We are talking about a lot of land—at least five thousand acres if we use the congressional criteria for wilderness—somehow left intact while several generations of resource-hungry people developed most of the continental landscape. We already know that a surprising number of such areas still exist but how far, for example, would a person living in New York City have to go to find such a place?

Backcountry areas that qualify under our definition survive in virtually every state and abound in all Canadian provinces. Our hypothetical Gotham City backcountry traveler has ample wild lands within an easy day's drive. He has a choice of the Berkshire Mountains to the east, the Adirondacks to the north, the Catskills to the west, and a number of backcountry areas in eastern Pennsylvania.

Our definition of backcountry, then, can range anywhere from a million sublime and terrifying acres of Montana's Bob Marshall Wilderness to 6,000 acres of rugged rolling hills in Missouri's Ozarks—anyplace that satisfies the requirements of remote, free-breathing size and undisturbed natural habitat.

Because the backcountry has survived by being tougher than the elements of society that would take off its rough edges and make it into something else, it is also tougher than most hunters and fishermen. Most people who hunt and fish have rather confined notions of the practice of their sport. Big game hunting is normally seen as a function of a well-organized roadhead camp with a large tent, three-burner stove, cots, and a walled privy. Fishing and bird hunting are either day trip affairs or protracted car camps with all of the amenities.

The backcountry hunter or fisherman is going to have to find a new vision of himself and his sport. He is going to have to reconcile himself to the trade-off between increased access to fish and game which the backcountry provides and the austerity the backcountry demands. Everything he needs to survive and pursue his sport will normally be carried on his back, and his range into the backcountry will depend on how well he can carry and use this limited equipment. The backcountry experience does not begin at dawn, break at noon, and end at dusk; it is a total sporting existence that lasts every minute of every day and night spent in the wilds.

But the rewards for the well but tightly equipped and properly conditioned sportsman far exceed the investments. The experience of being alone and truly on your own in the primal backcountry world is, as any backpacker can tell you, more than sufficient reward. Backpacking has caught on nationwide because it offers people a unique relationship between their bodies, their senses, and the land.

There is more in the backcountry for the hunter and fisherman, however, than the satisfaction of being there; there is a lost continent of unwary quarry. For the most part backcountry lakes and streams are peopled with wild fish which never have seen the inside of a hatchery and seldom have felt the barb of a fisherman's fly. They are plentiful, hungry, and easily beguiled.

And backcountry birds and game are not only more abundant back where the trails are thin, they are also less conditioned to the ways and wiles of men. That is why it is worth the trouble for hunters and fishermen to take their sport into the backcountry.

Taking your body and mind into the backcountry is undoubtedly good for both. But there are dangers and not all of them are of the physical, falling-off-a-cliff variety. Some of these hidden pitfalls attack the comfortable way we trinket-oriented Americans deal with our world while others plant new anxieties in our already overburdened minds.

There is, for instance, a condition which could best be designated as "backcountry neurosis." It eventually afflicts everybody who develops a keenness for unspoiled land.

The condition is manifested by an anxious, even desperate, compulsion to log as much time in the bush as possible while it still exists. The malaise is brought on by the realization that nothing is sacred in the United States, especially dormant land and resources easily converted into a quick buck. Knowing this, backcountry neurotics try to cram a lifetime's experience into every moment they can spend in the bush.

The problem is our technological society has an upsetting way of changing the ground rules about the worth of resources and how they can be exploited. Areas that were backcountry last year because nobody could figure out a way of making money by turning them into something else are clear-cut deserts, open pit mines, or suburbs today because somebody found a way. Lumber, fossil fuels, metals, and living space are becoming rarer and consequently more valuable. Corporations and agencies, having exhausted easily accessible resources, are now turning an eye toward these rugged backcountry enclaves and developing economically feasible means to dig deeper and cut higher to get the stubborn value out of wild lands. Technology has a way of leveling all obstacles.

Most people reading this book are probably already either hunters and fishermen or backpackers. Most will have experienced the soul-wrenching phenomenon of setting out into a favorite wild area where the trails were thin and the creatures foolish—only to find that somebody had been there ahead of them and left a power line, a dam, a highway, a mine, or a subdivision.

Several years ago I worked for a press service in Albany, New York. I wasn't exactly a green country kid with patched trousers, but my exposure to cities had been brief and I still had a farm boy's appreciation of a world of fresh air and green growing things. As cities go, I guess, Albany is all right, but to me there was something insipid and even a little frightening about acres of concrete and asphalt.

So on weekends, I would hitch up a pack and a fishing rod and explore the surrounding landscape for trout and the renewal of body and soul. One of my favorite places was a series of hills and high ridges along the Massachusetts border. I could climb one of these and lose myself for an entire weekend following the catacomb of intersecting hills.

There were several streams that welled in the maze of ridges where I could catch fish; hidden valleys where I could disappear into time and place, where the world and I seemed to be rotating in opposite directions, and majestic overviews looking down on the timeless charm and serenity of the Hudson Valley.

Although I dealt with the cold hard facts of politics, wars, and tragedies daily on my job, I felt that these weekends among the patient upper Hudson River ridges were the only link between me and reality. Without them I probably would have lost my body and my mind, if not my soul.

Then one Saturday afternoon I climbed into the hills after an especially brutal morning at the office when the entire world seemed to be burning and bludgeoning itself to death on the tele-type machines. Reaching the peak of the hill, I took one look behind me to say good-bye to the world's troubles and turned around to welcome the womb of the wilderness.

But I discovered the world's problems had followed me. A crew of hard-hatted construction workers were busily erecting a structure on the summit of the ridge from parts they had brought up a road newly engraved along the shoulder of the hill. The structure was to be a radio signal reflector because there were not enough radio signals around as it was. They would leave the road behind as a permanent breach for the outside world to attack my sanctuary.

I went through the motions of my weekend ritual but neither the fish nor the land were the same. Shortly after that I returned to Montana with a terminal case of backcountry neurosis.

However, I found the West offers only temporary symptomatic relief, like a bottle of aspirin. Although there are numerous wilderness areas, national parks, and vast ranges of unfettered backcountry, the rate of exploitation here is far greater than it is in the East, where most available resources have already been tapped. In the West, coal strip miners pile up a mountain of scraped earth in one place while mineral miners dismantle a mountain in another. Backcountry here is so ephemeral you almost need a score card to keep up with who is doing what to your favorite places.

There are a lot of people who spend a lot of time, intelligence, and energy fighting to keep wild places wild, and once in a while they win a round or two. But it isn't a fair fight and the erosion of wild lands goes on inexorably.

For one thing, preservationists are usually amateurs, taking time off from work and spending money out of their own pockets to go through the process of saving backcountry lands. The exploiters, on the other hand, are professionals who are paid handsomely by the taxpayers or consumers to spend as much time and money as is necessary to exploit the backcountry.

The weapons in the battle are selected by and favor the exploiter. Developers, foresters, and miners can translate their arguments into precise quantities: dollars, pounds, board feet, and jobs—the language land management agencies are conditioned to understand.

Preservationists, on the other hand, are usually restricted to talking about qualities. Hunting, fishing, backpacking, wildlife habitat, and other nonexploitive uses are resistant to precise quantification, putting preservationists at a real disadvantage when land managers begin their balancing act on the fate of backcountry lands. It is easier and safer to bureaucrats and politicians to base their decisions on cold, hard numbers than to take a chance on trying to justify nonproductive qualities. That is why there is such an enormous erosion of backcountry lands.

But numbers can be turned against the exploiters of the backcountry if the numbers reflect votes. The only really effective tool hunters, fishermen, and backpackers have is political pressure. If enough of them get together and make enough noise, somebody is going to hear and take notice.

Using the backcountry as a hunter, a fisherman, or just a hiker is not just a matter of a tidy pack and a firm pace, it is a total commitment to the land which will involve a lot of spare time and effort. It will mean going to land use hearings, testifying, writing letters to your state's congressional delegation and organizing other people who use the backcountry. All these activities are as important to the backcountry experience as landing a three-pound fish in an alpine lake, bagging a six-point buck by a marshy beaver pond, or reflecting on the timeless beauty of a flower-strewn mountain meadow.

CHAPTER 1

Basic Gear

Just about anything that is reasonably packable, provides shelter from the elements, and keeps you adequately warm will do as backcountry camping equipment. This can include stout but heavy G.I. surplus gear, official Boy Scout equipment of your youth, or the modern, lightwear equipment used for backpacking and mountaineering.

All three types of camping equipment will work but, fond as our society is of antiques and memorabilia, the veterans of ancient wars or the toys of our happy childhood are simply not as satisfactory as modern good-quality backpacking equipment.

Synthetic technology and aerodynamic engineering have combined to improve the quality of modern backpacking equipment. There is little question that modern boots, tents, sleeping bags, stoves, and raingear are lighter, more compact, warmer, longer-lasting (with care), and more efficient than their counterparts of twenty or thirty years ago.

Modern backpacking gear began to evolve shortly after the

Second World War when petrochemical synthetics such as nylon and dacron became available and a small but growing market of backpackers and mountaineers began to insist on better-quality, lightweight gear. Through the years this market has grown exponentially and along with it has grown an entire industry—from hundreds of small shops which barely make the yellow pages to Dun and Bradstreet-listed firms catering to the demands of backcountry enthusiasts.

This market, now estimated at about 20 million people, has created a demand for the services of hundreds of clever engineers and designers in developing refinements in materials and performance. Small basement operations have expanded into modest manufacturing shops which are now offering the best outdoor equipment ever made.

But these modern wonders of light weight and efficiency are expensive and getting more so every year. In 1977 it would cost a minimum of about $300 to outfit one person in good-quality spring-, summer-, and fall-weight gear. Add another $100 to bolster that to all-season service and then double the figure if you want the very best, lightest-weight, and most elegant equipment.

Most hunters and fishermen already have some of the gear they will need for backcountry expeditions. Most, for instance, already have some kind of sleeping bag and, although it may not be the latest state of the art, light as a feather and fluffy as a pillow, it can be made to do until a rich uncle dies. Other gear such as pocketknives, sheath knives, hunting compasses, tarps, hunting boots, and an old army rucksack will also suffice. But remember this stuff weighs several times what modern special-purpose equipment does, and weight is the chief restriction in range and comfort of backcountry travel.

Remember, too, you will not only have to lug your camping and hiking gear in your quest for backcountry quarry but also the means of pursuing the quarry. Big game hunters can count on at least an additional ten pounds in special gear necessary for the stalk, wildfowl hunters probably nearly as much, and fishing or photography can call for four or five pounds of extra baggage.

When you add the tools that are necessary to pursue backcountry sport to the hiking and camping equipment required, an investment in lightweight modern equipment makes more sense.

Let's consider these equipment options in relation to the shoulder blades, the part of your anatomy that will probably feel most of the weight. You hear and read a lot about people skipping through the wilderness with seventy-pound loads on their backs and smiles on their faces. These tales may be true, but I think either their scale or their sanity should be certified. I am big, nearly two hundred pounds, fairly young and in good hiking condition, and a fifty-pound load on my back is about as much as I would care to tote while having fun.

Further, I would personally not even consider carrying as much as fifty pounds on hunting trips for any reason short of a gun in my back. It is just entirely too much weight; too much energy and attention must be concentrated on supporting the load and not enough can be spared for the more important task of looking for an animal. My own weight limit for a three-day big game hunting trip is thirty-five pounds. I will add a few pounds for extended wildfowl or fishing trips, but only with reluctance.

I feel that thirty-five pounds is as much as I can carry and still be agile enough to dodge sticks and twigs, light-footed enough to avoid rattling stones, and attentive enough to my surroundings to watch for game (I don't see any point in walking through prime big game habitat, which is what you are doing when you are heading into the backcountry, without hunting it).

Now let's measure my thirty-five-pound pack against the total weight of Army surplus and vintage camping gear. An Army featherback mummy bag weighs about six pounds without wool liner or cotton cover. Conventional rectangular sleeping bags weigh much more, up to about ten pounds. Boy Scout, Army surplus, and old-fashioned floorless pup tents weight about five pounds without stakes or mosquito protection. Vinylized fabric waterproofs weigh another three pounds. A wool or conventionally insulated heavy fabric jacket is another five pounds in the pack and by the time you add an extra change of clothes and the necessary miscellaneous camping items (stove, compass, first aid kit, rope, maps, and canteen), you will have another seven or eight pounds. With the three to five pounds of food necessary for our three-day stalk you have a minimum weight of thirty pounds on your back, not including the weight of the pack.

Now include the weight of your Army surplus rucksack (five

pounds) and the ten pounds of hunting equipment and you will find yourself stumbling under forty-five pounds of dead weight. I maintain that nobody can stalk through forests or marshes with that kind of load on his shoulders.

On the other hand, keeping your hunting pack down to a tidy thirty-five pounds is not much of a problem with lightweight backpacking gear. My three-season sleeping bag weighs three pounds; my tent, complete with floor, mosquito protection, and hardware, weighs a little less than six pounds. My waterproof poncho weighs about half a pound and my down jacket less than a pound. The miscellaneous lightweight gear comes to a tad less than four pounds, including extra pants, a shirt, and three days' worth of freeze-dried trail food which weighs about three pounds. The total weight of my pack contents comes to seventeen and one-half pounds and actually I would be much better equipped for foul weather than my brave, surplus-equipped counterpart. Adding the weight of my pack, two and one-half pounds, and my obligatory ten pounds of hunting equipment, I still have five pounds left over for fluff and comfort (which I don't have any trouble filling).

The point is that you can get away with lugging heavy, old-fashioned equipment into the backcountry, but you are better off in terms of both weight and efficiency with more expensive but better-designed modern gear.

Let's take a look at the things you will need to get into and stay out in the backcountry. All of these things are standard for backcountry travel, regardless of whether you are hunting, fishing, taking pictures, or just gawking. As we go, let's measure the options against one another and try to decide where the prospective backcountry traveler should invest his money to get the most out of it.

BOOTS

I don't think there is any doubt that good, well-fitted, and appropriately designed boots are the most important piece of backcountry equipment you need. Regardless of whether you are traveling the mountains or the marshes, whether you are getting there by foot, horseback, skis, or canoe, your footwear should be the best you can afford.

For mountain travel there is only one choice: leather, Vibram-soled, padded-ankle mountain boots. Vibram soles are thick composition rubber molded into a lug pattern which is designed to grip rocks. Any boot without a Vibram or Vibram-type composition sole is not only tiresome but actually downright dangerous in the mountains.

Our mountain travel boot must be built on Vibram soles but how about Vibram-soled hunting boots or Vietnam surplus boots? A well-soled hunting boot might fill the requirements of a mountain boot provided it can be waterproofed to shed snow and endure shallow creek crossings and has enough support in the ankles and instep to protect your feet. Most do not and should be rejected but if your hunting boots have heavily padded ankles and a firm arch support, they will probably do. Vietnam boots do not have the necessary support and were literally designed to drink water.

Hiking and mountaineering boots (the difference is primarily a matter of support reflected in weight) are made to not only give you sure footing in rocky, mountainous terrain but also to bolster your ankles and instep under heavy weights. Your feet, like most of your body, have developed to function only under average stresses and strains. When you add another twenty-five to thirty pounds to your body weight and move it over rough country, your ankles and feet are going to need some help. Good hiking boots and mountaineering boots are designed to provide just that, insulating the bottoms of your feet against bruising by sharp rocks, supporting the arch and instep, and binding the ankle so that it can't twist sideways in the boot.

I think the $50 to $75 good hiking or mountaineering boots cost is a wise investment for mountain travel; so consider them a major necessity if your backcountry travels will take you into the mountains.

For most three-season mountain travel, you are better off with lighter good-quality hiking boots than with the rigid and somewhat clumsy mountaineering boots.

Hiking boots have become something of a fad, and the market offers many so-called hiking boots which are either too light for load-bearing or too poorly made to hold up under the rigors of mountain travel. There are several ways of telling the good and useful from the not so good and useless. A first requirement is enough substance to hold up, and this can be measured in weight. Most makers list the weight of various models as "average weight." If the average weight of the model you are looking at is under three and one-half pounds, it may not have enough back-bone.

Next look at how the soles are connected to the uppers. Your backcountry mountain boots should have a midsole of leather or composition stitched to the uppers. There are three acceptable methods of stitching: (1) the Norwegian welt, which is the strongest and heaviest and consists of two or three rows of stitches on the outside of the welt; (2) the Goodyear seam, which has two rows of stitching on the outside and is lighter, and (3) the Littleway stitch, which has no visible stitching on the outside. If you look inside the boot, you will see two rows of stitches holding the uppers to the midsole. This is the lightest acceptable method and is now used on most good lightweight hiking boots.

While you are looking inside the boot, look at the lining. Does it extend all the way around the toe? Beware of buying boots that are not fully lined. I have seen (and worn) too many pairs with only ankle lining which disintegrated all too quickly.

The ankle lining conceals foam padding on all hiking boots. Check this sandwich affair to make sure it is firm and well anchored to the outside of the boot. The ankle lining should also be stitched, not glued, to the toe lining.

Most hiking boots have a padded collar around the top to keep stones, snow, and detritus out of the boot. This "scree collar" should fit snugly around the ankles but ought not to be too high or fluffy; otherwise, it will be exposed to chafing and wear.

My lightweight hiking boots, made by Pivetta, are Italian boots with a Littleway welt and weigh less than four pounds on my size eleven feet. They are amply ridged around my ankles but yet allow enough flex in the soles to complement what is left of my youthful bounce. They cost about $65.

For snow or heavier mountain travel I wear a pair of Lowa Alpspitz. Their five and one-half pounds of bulk and brawn have stood up under five years and hundreds of really tough miles.

They are not as pleasant to walk in as the twinkle-toe Pivettas but there have been times in numbing cold and among thin rock holds that their weight has paid off handsomely. The Alpspitz cost about $75.

Marshlands require really specialized footgear. In the flats of central Michigan, in Arkansas and Illinois there is a lot of backcountry that has escaped the madding crowds because it is spongy and damp and most people don't like to get their feet wet. In areas where you are constantly walking in water it is impractical, if not impossible, to keep feet dry. You can wear hip boots or farmer's rubber boots, but constant walking in these stuffy boilers will produce enough sweat and condensation to soak your feet. And, because of the loose slip-over fit, these boots would make raw meat out of your feet in a couple of miles.

There are only two seasonal alternatives for the marshlands, which offer some of the best backcountry wild hunting and fishing imaginable. In the summer wear footwear which dries nearly as quickly as it soaks, such as fabric high-top sneakers or Vietnam boots. Vietnam Army boots cost about the same as sneakers, $12 to $14, and are well designed to cope with soggy lowlands. They have a stout Vibram sole, leather bottoms with one-way drain valves, and nylon uppers which are cool and dry quickly.

Winter is a different problem. In temperatures hovering around freezing, wet feet are a pain or worse, and you can't rely on ice to hold you up. Packs are probably the best way to go, either the all-rubber kind or the more expensive rubber bottom, leather top variety. I don't get along well with the all-rubber kind because my feet sweat profusely and I end up sloshing inside my boots after three or four miles. I prefer a rubber sole with a water-resistant leather top such as the L. L. Bean Maine boot. This type of boot offers enough protection against outside water if you are nimble and yet allows your feet to transpire most excess inside moisture through the leather uppers. Bean and similar good-quality packs cost from $40 to $50, depending on the length of the uppers and tread design.

Other types of terrain such as forested hills, plains, and deserts are easier on the feet and therefore easier to buy boots for. Reasonably good-quality hunting boots, packs (in winter),

Basic Backcountry Boots

Upper left is a standard hunting boot by Browning. This kind of boot is adequate for mild terrain and modest backpacking loads. Upper right is famous L. L. Bean Maine boot. Waterproof to the ankle and highly water-resistant through the calf, the Maine boot is ideal for marshes, swamps, and wet snow. Lower left is a light hiking boot by Pivetta. The boots are light and nimble yet stout enough to hold up under heavy loads on all but the ruggedest mountain trails. Lower right is the Lowa Alpspitz, a heavy mountaineering boot for treacherous off-trail mountain travel.

surplus boots with good soles (watch out for leather bottoms in the snow), or even tennis shoes (in the summer) will do. But I prefer a pair of good-quality light hiking boots even in easy terrain if just for the added ankle support.

Boots are the most important piece of backcountry gear you need; so choose them carefully and plan to spend as much as you can afford.

BACKPACKS

I am somewhat reluctant to elevate backpacks to the number two equipment priority but we are discussing gear on the basis of cost-benefit and if all you have is an old-fashioned pack, you can get a lot of benefit out of a little investment.

Rucksacks, both the Army surplus and Boy Scout old-fashioned commercial varieties, weigh altogether more than they should in the first place and also manage, by a miracle of distorted leverage, to double the weight of any load. Conversely, modern load-bearing backpacks, even cheap imports, manage to make loads feel lighter than their actual weight.

There are essentially two different kinds of backpacks available today which can manage the bulk and weight necessary for backcountry hunting and fishing trips. The most common is the external metal frame, which distributes the weight of a well-packed bag evenly between the shoulders and hips. A new concept in backpacks uses a soft sack and spreads the weight evenly along the back between the hips and shoulders. Some of these new packs use anatomically designed internal fiberglass or metal frames, while others are designed to form their own frames as you fill them with equipment.

Frame packs have several advantages. First of all, they are absolutely rigid and therefore hold their shape and retain their weight-distributing quality even under very heavy loads. They are extremely popular, having become more or less the mark of an outdoorsman, and consequently are available in a wide variety of sizes, shapes, and prices. Prices range from about $25 for a marginally serviceable import to well over $100 for a sophisticated heavyweight pack designed for Himalayan mountain travel. About $50 will buy a frill-less but stout American-made frame pack that will hold up under reasonable loads and last many seasons. I have a Kelty frame that is ten years old and has been around the world. It is still quite serviceable although I have retired it to the relatively minor function of hauling quartered big game out of the hills.

The Kelty is living a soft life these days because I discovered the self-forming soft pack about five years ago. These frameless, large-volume packs were developed by the Rivendell Mountain Works of Victor, Idaho about a decade ago to provide mountain climbers and cross-country skiers with a more graceful way of hauling equipment through rough country.

The self-forming frame system starts with a soft pack which is divided into columns, usually three. A bottom, horizontal column is jammed with soft gear such as sleeping bags to form the foundation of the pack. Then two vertical top columns are packed to form a kind of gothic arch over the foundation, and the pack becomes a rigid structure. Loaded properly, the pack can carry thirty-five to forty pounds of gear more easily than any other form of pack because its low sectional profile blends into back, shoulders, and hips.

The advantages of this pack structure are not only reflected in the easy carrying of moderately heavy loads but also in the unobtrusive low profile. There is no awkward bulge or ungainly extension to catch on brush or rocks; and the pack moves with the flow of the body rather than requiring the hiker to adjust to the restrictions of the pack, as in the case of frame packs.

Obviously this kind of pack is appreciated by mountaineers and should be equally useful to wilderness sportsmen, especially hunters. The same freedom mountaineers enjoy with self-forming soft packs gives big game hunters a better opportunity to still-hunt quietly while backpacking on the trail.

Some soft packs have internal frames. They range from sleazy, but sometimes elegant-looking, imported rucksacks to really serious and expensive expedition affairs. Most of the imports are rather witless variations on the ancient rucksack theme with malleable aluminum stays running up the back and along the hips. The better internal frames are designed wide and flat with compressor straps on the outside to bring the load as close to the back as the frame will allow. Frames in better-quality internally supported packs are either bendable metal or contour-forming fiberglass.

There are several problems with internal frame packs which tend to reduce them, at best, to a compromise between external frame packs and self-forming soft packs. In the first place the frame, no matter how thin or well-designed, tends to push the load away from the back with the loss of that "shirt on your back" feeling the frameless soft packs give. Also, without the vertical columns, loads tend to bulge toward the center, pushing the center of weight farther away from your center of balance.

On the other hand, better internal frame packs will carry heavier loads than the frameless and give you a more graceful carry than a frame pack.

I feel that self-forming soft packs are the best adapted to the needs of the backcountry sportsman. They carry all the weight you need more comfortably than the other two; they put that weight around the back where it is least likely to upset your balance while thrashing through the brush, clambering over rocks, or stalking, and they allow enough clearance in back for a slung rifle or strapped-on fishing rod.

The price range of self-forming packs is about the same as for the two framed packs. That is, you can buy an adequate soft pack from several makers for about $50. However, if you want the combination of quality and capacity that will iron out the thirty-five-pound backcountry load we are talking about, you might be wise to spend half again as much. For years I used a Rivendell Jensen pack. It would hold just about anything I wanted to put in it and carried like a feather. Two years ago I swapped it for a Chouinard Ultima Thule, which carries nearly as well as the Jensen but has the capacity to carry more than I usually care to lug. The Thule is top-opening, which allows it to carry considerably more than 4,000 cubic inches; the Jensen uses a clever back-opening zipper, which restricts it to somewhat less than 4,000 cubic inches. Both currently cost about $75.

TENTS

Pup tents, tarps, and nylon flies work fine for late spring, summer, and early fall excursions. Properly pitched, any of these will protect you from showers and chilly mountain breezes and cost but a trifle. However, if you are camping in mosquito country or plan to extend your sporting excursions into the late fall or winter, you had better consider a tent.

Backpacking tents range in price from $35 for discount house import specials to $300 for Himalayan high-altitude expedition models. In size, accommodations vary from cramped two-person wedges to luxurious four- and even five-person affairs.

I don't feel the average backcountry sportsman should seriously consider either end of the price span. Cheap tents are just that, poorly made from inadequate materials. They always have waterproofed canopies (as opposed to porous tops with waterproof fly covers) which sweat and swelter in the summer and snow frozen condensation on occupants in colder weather.

On the other hand, top-of-the-line expedition tents are bolstered in cost and weight to withstand the worst this earth can throw at them. Using one of these for normal conditions would be like grocery shopping in a Mack truck.

The capacity of your backcountry tent is another matter, however. Multiperson tents actually cost and weigh less per person than smaller two-person tents. A ten-pound, $200 four-man tent, for instance, comes out to two and one-half pounds per person and $50 a head; whereas a comparable quality two-man tent that costs $150 and weighs six pounds amounts to $75 and three pounds of carry weight per sleeper.

The point is, if you are sure you will be backcountrying with three or four persons most of the time, a single large tent is a better buy than more than one smaller tent.

I do most of my backpacking and backcountry sporting either by myself or with well-equipped companions. Therefore I have no need for a tent larger than a two-person and have stuck with that size for the past fifteen years. For ten of those years I have used a 5½-pound Gerry Year Rounder (which in current models weighs six pounds and costs $150) during the spring and fall or when I pitch summer camps in mosquito country. It has been most of the way around the world with me. I recently calculated that I have spent over a thousand nights under it. And, I have no doubt, with proper care I will spend another thousand nights in it.

For late fall hunting season and winter camping I use a heavier

Gerry called the Mountain II. It weighs three pounds more than the Year Rounder but has the substance to withstand harsh conditions and the size to make sitting out storms tolerable. It has most of the conveniences of home including a zippered urinal, cookhole in the floor, and a tunnel "porch" for getting out of wet clothes. It currently costs about $200.

Recently I have been using a tent which may answer the requirements of the weight-conscious fair weather hiker as well as the late season hunter hiker. It is called the Bombshelter and is made by Rivendell Mountain Works of Victor, Idaho. At six pounds total weight it is certainly the lightest heavy-duty tent available.

It is designed for winter, high-altitude camping with two A-frames which cant toward the middle supported by a stout aluminum ridgepole. The lightweight nylon tent and fly fabric covers this stout aluminum foundation like a lean skin, making the tent as wind- and snow-resistant as a tent can be.

There are a couple of comfort and convenience trade-offs for all this strength, however. Being primarily designed as a winter tent, the Bombshelter has only one entrance and that is a long tunnel. Tunnels are necessary in bad weather and snow to give campers a place to shed wet, snowy clothing and extricate themselves from morning snowdrifts. During the spring, summer, and fall, however, a tunnel is just an awkward way of getting in and out. The main drawback of the Bombshelter is its interior size. The width of the floor is only forty-five inches, making it positively indecent for two large men. However, solos and couples might find it an ideal lightweight indestructible shelter for all types of weather if they can afford the $200 price tag.

PONCHOS

Waterproofs are one item in the backcountry outfit where a little money goes a long way. Common garden variety fishing and hunting raingear just simply can't hack it in the backcountry. It is designed for fashion and a rather limited specific purpose and is too delicate, too vulnerable, too confining, and much too heavy.

All of these deficiencies in sporting waterproofs make the $15 to $25 laid out for a backpacker's poncho the only real bargain

Lightweight Mountain Tent

Shown here is a Rivendell Bombshelter, so named because once pitched it is practically impossible for weather conditions to knock it down. It is a remarkably light (six pounds complete) two-person shelter which does everything a tent should— protect against rain, wind, snow, and bugs.

you are going to get while equipping yourself for backcountry sport.

Ponchos are a bargain because there is so little to them and because nearly all of the hundreds of backpacking manufacturers market them. They consist merely of a rectangular piece of water-proofed nylon with a hole cut in the middle. Most have hoods over the holes, some just collars. All are large enough to drape completely over the average human body, covering down to the knees in front and back and out to the elbows on the sides. Some are cut extralong in the back to compensate for the hump the pack makes. Most ponchos are made of either nylon taffeta, which is extremely abrasion- and tear-resistant, or ripstop nylon, which is more delicate but lighter and therefore more compact. I prefer taffeta because ponchos are subject to quite a beating.

Ponchos are wonderful not only because they will keep rain and soggy brush water off hikers better than any other garment but also because they can be used for several other purposes. They can be snapped and tucked all around you for a watertight sitting shelter while waiting out a heavy storm. They are a good water-proof groundcloth for sleeping under the stars or adding a water barrier under your tent. Some are large enough to be folded over and snapped to make a waterproof sleeping bag bivouac. Two small ones or one large one can make an adequate shelter-half tent. A poncho can also be used as an emergency litter for an accident victim.

The tougher taffeta ponchos tend to last forever. I am still using a Kelty poncho I bought in 1968 and, although the water-proofing has worn a little thin in spots, it still keeps me tolerably dry.

There are other forms of backpacking waterproofs, such as full-length cagoules and waterpants or the new GoreTex parkas, but they are considerably more expensive than ponchos, won't keep you any drier (if as dry), and don't have any of the added benefits. Buy a poncho.

SLEEPING BAGS

A sleeping bag must have enough loft to keep you warm during the seasons you intend to be in the backcountry. In addition, the bag should be designed to be light and compact as well as warm.

You may already have a bag which meets the absolute requirement of warmth and feel the $60 to $150 necessary to upgrade the system is not worth it. The old feather Army surplus bags or camper sleeping robes with down, kapok, or early synthetic fills might do if you don't mind tilting your pack with bulky loads that are usually twice as heavy as need be. I know a lot of experienced hikers and backcountry hunters and fishermen who have somehow managed to put up with chicken quills and other assorted ordnance poking through the linings of war surplus bags for many years. I also know people who can't stand to sleep in confining mummy-shaped bags and don't seem to mind hauling around eight pounds of rectangular nocturnal luxury. But if you are going to go either of these economy routes, remember that it will cost you two to five pounds of dead weight and bulk, which translates into reduced mobility and energy on the trail.

If you want to go first class, there are essentially two options in modern lightweight mummy or semimummy bags: down or synthetics. Goose down is the standard insulator of backpacking bags. It is light, lofty, resilient, and compressible. It is also horribly expensive. Goose down bags currently cost from $100 to $200. Duck down does everything goose down will do, only not quite so well, and costs not quite so much.

Modern synthetic insulators do not loft as well as the downs for their weight and can't be compressed into as small a package, but have some advantages including price. For one thing, the three currently being used—PolarGuard, Fibrefill II, and Holofil—are all nearly 100 percent nonabsorbent, which means they dry quickly and are warm even when wet. Down is next to useless if it is wet and takes forever to dry.

The synthetics, unlike down, also provide some compressed insulation, which means the bottom of the bag will protect you somewhat from the cold, hard earth.

The synthetics are considerably cheaper than down, from about one-third to two-thirds the cost for a given amount of insulation.

The quantity of insulation in a sleeping bag is best measured in terms of total loft of the bag, although some makers still talk in terms of the total weight of insulation. One problem with weight-oriented measurement is that different bag configurations will result in different insulating values obtained from the same total weight of insulator. For instance, a semirectangular bag will not be neary as warm with two pounds of insulation as would a more space-efficient tight mummy design with the same amount of insulation. Not to mention the difference between two pounds of goose down as opposed to two pounds of PolarGuard.

When you buy a bag, either down or synthetic, look for loft measurement. This rating irons out the difference between the different types of insulation and styles of cut and configuration. It will give you a precise idea of how warm the bag will be.

If you intend to restrict your backcountry activities to the three temperate seasons, a bag with five inches of loft from bottom to top will probably keep you warm down to freezing. If you are tall and lean with a low metabolism, you might consider adding half an inch or so. Conversely, if you are compactly built, you might find five inches too warm at times.

For early spring and late fall outings where nighttime temperatures might get down as low as zero, a fatter bag or some additional insulation for your light bag may be necessary. At zero most people need at least seven inches of loft to stay cozy. However, a seven-inch bag might be a tad balmy in the summer.

There are a number of ways of bolstering the loft of a sleeping bag. The two simplest are: (1) taking along a quilt and folding it or tucking it around the bag, or (2) wearing enough clothing to bed to make up the necessary amount of insulation. I prefer the latter course because a quilt is just so much dead weight in the pack while extra clothing can always be justified as replacements for wet garments or adding comfort to chilly evenings in camp.

This extra bed clothing should consist of a pair or two of dry, clean wool socks or insulated booties; long johns, either fishnet, thermal cotton, wool, or quilted, depending on how underinsulated you expect your bag to be; and a down or wool jacket. All of these garments can be used for emergency or luxury clothing as well as supplemental sleeping loft.

I own two sleeping bags. A 3¾-pound PolarGuard-insulated 5-inch loft bag for temperate weather and a 4½-pound goose down bag with 7 inches of loft for winter.

The synthetic is a cleverly engineered offset quilt design by Camp Trails which gives me three inches of loft on top and two on

Lightweight Semimummy Sleeping Bag

A sleeping bag must have enough insulation to retain body heat under current temperature conditions. This bag from Camp Trails weighs three pounds, ten ounces and has PolarGuard synthetic insulation.

the bottom. Although down bags with equivalent loft would be somewhat lighter, I like the PolarGuard for the rainy season because I can crawl into it wet and still enjoy a clammy warmth.

The bag is called the Sandarac and currently costs about $60, which is about half the price of a light down bag.

In the winter, when weight and bulk become a consideration, I feel the relative efficiency of down is worth the price. I use a Sierra Designs four-season bag which has taken the nip off many mountain winter nights.

Although there is a considerable weight and loft difference between the two bags, both compress into about the same area of my pack, which makes pack planning a lot easier both summer and winter.

CLOTHING

Wool is probably still the best all-around insulator for a working body. It is an excellent insulator for its given loft. Tightly woven wool breaks winds and prevents heat loss through convection (disturbance of dead air). Good weaves shed water like a duck, and all wool garments will continue to provide warmth even when wet. Wool is durable, common, and not especially expensive. Most experienced hikers would not consider going on a day hike, in July, without at least a wool sweater or shirt in their pack. Wool is probably the foundation material for all backcountry clothing needs.

However, the range of day-to-day and season-to-season temperature variations, weather conditions, and stresses and strains on the body are going to require more than one garment made from more than one material in the backcountry. The key to comfort and safety in the backcountry is modular, or "layered," clothing.

Layering means the hiker has a variety of clothing to choose from which can be worn either singly or in combination with other clothing to meet changing conditions. A good place to start building these layers is next to the skin with appropriate underwear. Swedish "fishnet" underwear is probably the best year-round choice. Its one-quarter- to one-eighth-inch mesh is cool in the summer and allows perspiration to escape from the body

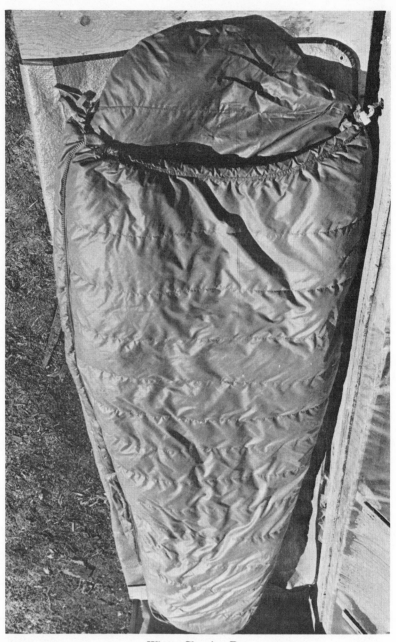

Winter Sleeping Bag

This is a full mummy-cut goose down bag by Sierra Designs which will keep most people cozy at well below zero.

without dampening outer clothing. In colder weather the fishnet creates small dead air cells between the body and outer garments, adding insulation and preventing perspiration buildup.

During the temperate seasons a sleeveless sweatshirt will break breezes, provide a little warmth, and dry quickly. Tennis or walking shorts are nice during the heat of the day and can be topped off with a pair of cotton pants or blue jeans when things start to cool.

During the summer a wool sweater is usually sufficient to keep out the evening or morning chills. I also like to carry a down vest or light down jacket for a pillow and for unseasonable chills.

In the fall the down jacket becomes standard equipment in my pack along with an extra pair of lightweight wool pants or knickers and a second wool sweater or shirt. During the fall, then, I am sometimes wearing as many as four layers of clothing—net underwear, sweatshirt, wool sweater and down jacket on top with fishnet drawers, shorts, and wool pants on the bottom. During warm Indian summer days most of this can be stripped off, and during chilly harvest moon evenings I can put all or most of it back on.

During the three temperate seasons waterproofs are absolutely essential. A drenching decreases the insulating properties of all the clothing layers and can leave you essentially naked to the cold.

During the winter waterproofs are probably not necessary in most areas (although winter thaws and rains are celebrated killers in the Southeast and on the Pacific Coast), but you will need a lot more pucker in outer clothing. Sitting around in camp or bivouacking during late fall hunting season or winter can require as much as three inches of body insulation for the torso. Wool, the ideal insulator for milder climes, is just too heavy to meet cold weather needs. Although a wool sweater is excellent for a lower layer, you will need some kind of down or synthetically insulated parka as an overlayer.

The qualities of goose and duck down that make them the best insulators for winter bags also make them good for winter parkas. Down parkas now cost from about $50 for a run-of-the-mill single-layer jacket to $150 for a double-offset quilt expedition affair. Neither extreme is really suitable for the temperature range we are talking about.

Rather than attempting to meet all weather conditions with one down garment, I prefer to apply the layer principle to feathers as well as other clothing. In the late fall I carry both a lightweight down vest, made by Camp 7, and an orange medium-weight parka made by Woolrich. Together, they are sufficient to meet any turns for the worse and one or the other of them alone is enough to combat more ordinary cold weather. In the deep winter I exchange the vest for a North Face down jacket, which, when combined with the parka, is ample against the coldest winter nights.

Hands, feet, and heads are problems that tend to stand out in the cold. During the summer, good wool socks and an extra pair of sneakers are enough to keep toes nimble. The layer principle applies here too, although I always wear two pairs of socks between my feet and hiking boots no matter how warm it is. My favorite combination is cotton socks on the inside with a pair of heavy wool rag socks over them. The cotton wicks moisture away from my feet and provides a kind of frictionless bushing which cuts down wear, tear, and blistering. I always carry three pairs of each so I can alternate them between my feet, washing, and spares.

There is an old saying that if your feet are cold, cover your head. That is a pretty sage observation. Studies have shown that 70 to 80 percent of all heat lost by the body goes out the top of the head. This is because the brain has the greatest need for constant heat of any part of the body but has the least amount of body insulation to retain it. Consequently, in cold weather your body sends heat first to your head, which, if you don't provide head insulation, loses it practically as fast as it receives it. And while all this finite body heat is going to your head, other parts of your body are being deprived.

The obvious solution to this problem is to wear a hat; it really is as simple as that. Any hat or cap that provides both wind protection and insulation will do but some are more efficient than others. The best I know of is the wool knit Balaclava helmet, which not only protects the skull like a watch cap but also pulls down over the face and neck. Balaclavas are especially nice for big game hunters because a polyester blaze-orange watch cap can be sewed to the top, providing both an additional layer of warmth and the comforting reassurance that the top of your head does not resemble any part of a known game species.

In deep winter, the Balaclava, combined with the insulated hood on your parka, will provide the layers necessary to keep you warm in varying degrees of cold.

Although sleeping caps may be out of fashion in the boudoirs of civilization, a Balaclava pulled down tight around the neck can mean the difference between a snug night's rest and a chilling experience.

There are several Balaclavas available today, but for $5 you can't do better than a nicely woven cap by Wigwam Mills.

Hands are undoubtedly the toughest part of the anatomy to insulate properly. There is relatively little circulation through them and consequently it takes a great deal of insulation to retain the limited amount of heat they do generate. If you wear bulky fluffy mittens, you temporarily sacrifice the use of these marvelous tools but if you don't, you may lose the use of them permanently.

Most backcountry hunters and fishermen won't have to worry about frostbiting temperatures. Spring, summer, and fall fishermen may not need any protection for their hands at all. But in the mountains of northwestern Montana I find that a pair of fingerless palm socks can come in very handy during an April or August cold snap and don't take any more pack space than an extra T-shirt.

In the early spring and late fall, something a little more elaborate is usually wise. For the tangy cold of March or November I carry the palm socks for a foundation on which I can add a pair of wool mittens with an appendage trigger finger (essential for hunting) knitted in and a brace of fabric wind- and water-resistant shells to match. Both the Canadian and U.S. Army-made mittens and shells will fit the bill nicely for about $5.

During the hard bone-cracking winter, hands and fingers need a bit more than a couple of layers of wool. Although humankind has fashioned many technological wonders with its hands, it still has not devised a way of protecting them from the cold without resorting to mounds of fluff. Those two marvels of dexterity which have made us manipulators of the world are reduced to a pair of clumsy paws in winter. Big mittens are the only way we can cope with subzero cold.

In the past, the backpacker's solution to this has been down-filled or pile-lined mittens. Pile is only marginally adequate and down, for all of its cozy fluff, cannot insulate under compression. This means you are all right until you try to use something—a ski pole, rifle, or ice axe. Then the sharp cold of the implement bites through the glove into your hand.

The best solution is a synthetic, like PolarGuard, which insulates under compression. Rivendell has a pair of mittens and shells called "Hot Tomalis" which keep hands comfortable if not entirely functional, for about $30.

FOOD AND COOKING GEAR

Although nothing adds flavor to a backcountry expedition like a dinner of fresh-killed fare over the glowing embers of a wood fire, life in the wilderness doesn't always work that way. Back-country sportsmen will need to bring along ample food for the length of their trip and, in many cases, a means to cook it.

In many areas of the country, fires are prohibited during the summer season and several national parks have extended the ban year-around. In these areas you will need a light, efficient back-packer's stove. But stoves are handy for a number of other reasons and might be considered standard equipment for all backcountry jaunts. For one thing, a stove will always light and cook no matter how wet the wood is. For big-game hunters, stoves substantially reduce the human smells and sights that game animals instinctively avoid. A roaring fire in camp may warm the cockles of a hunter's heart but has the opposite effect on any game in the neighborhood.

There are basically two kinds of backpacker stoves available today: (1) those with burners that attach to disposable pressurized cartridges, and (2) self-contained gas, kerosene, and alcohol burners. Cartridge stoves are less expensive to buy (from $15 to $25) but expensive to feed, light but bulky (you normally have to carry two of the ungainly cartridges into the backcountry and out), and the spent cartridges present a disposal problem.

Cartridge stoves also lose efficiency in cold weather and at high altitudes.

On the other hand, self-contained stoves are getting horribly expensive ($25 to $45), are generally messier and harder to light, and are not as safe in closed areas. The heat-generating types of gas and alcohol stoves suffer the same high-altitude and cold-weather drawbacks as cartridge types. The pump-generated stoves are generally bulky and always expensive.

The best all-around stove I have found is the Mountain Safety Research Model Nine. It comes in two parts which can be carried separately: the pumper fuel storage bottle and the generator-burner. It burns fast and efficiently (boils a pint of water in less than three minutes), doesn't incur most of the mess and fuss associated with fuel stoves, and lights simply with the flick of a cigarette lighter flint. Using independent fuel bottles, it can store an enormous amount of stove or nonleaded automotive gas. The only drawback of the MSR is its cost, currently edging toward $45.

Food is a highly personal thing. Some people can eat mush day in, day out, for a week without their taste buds or stomach suffering. Most, however, require a bit more refinement and variety in their cuisine.

Until recently, variety in trail foods meant a lot of dead carrying weight in foods and cooking implements. The introduction of freeze-dried dinners has made wilderness dining reasonably elegant and carrying and preparing food light and simple. Oregon Freeze-Dry Foods, Inc., market a vast variety of nutritious and tasty snacks and dinners under a number of different labels. These weigh next to nothing and cook quickly in boiling water. They are, however, a bit more expensive, averaging about $1.50 a meal.

A cheaper but weightier, and usually less nutritious, alternative is food market dehydrated food. This includes soups, condiments, milk, cocoa, and texturized protein foods and mixes. Some of these are honest bargains, such as dried eggs, instant milk, some packaged soups, and granola cereals. Dehydrated milk and eggs go nicely with just about anything and should be a staple with all backcountry wanderers. One of my favorite dishes is those two mixed liberally with Chinese noodles; it makes a wholesome and tasty meal for two. Supermarket instant coffee, tea and cocoa are also staples which cost little and add a lot to back-country meals.

Granola cereals make a fine base for a hearty trail food. Add nuts and dried fruit and it goes well either by itself or with milk as a trail snack. For breakfast I like packaged sweetened oatmeal because it is filling, somewhat nourishing, and easy to fix.

Perhaps the nicest thing about freeze-dried foods is the fact that all they require is boiled water—nothing to cook them in and no serving dishes. This means all the hiker needs to carry is a one-pint pot or so to boil water. This is especially critical to big game hunters because it means fewer things to rattle and clang in the pack and a stealthier stalk. Anything, even something as simple as a G.I. canteen cup, will put freeze-drieds on the table.

Dehydrated foods are a different story. They have to be cooked in a pan or pot and eaten out of something; so the investment in hardware is going to be higher. The tried and trusted Boy Scout individual cook set with small fry pan, plate, cup, and one-pint pot will handle most tasks within reason. However, one of the many variations on the theme with a larger, fancier fry pan may be better if you are inclined toward more elaborate menus.

No matter what you take in the way of multiple pot and pan sets, make sure they nest tightly by adding shims of scouring cloth, pieces of soap, or spare matches. This hardware will be nuisance enough as it is without providing game with an advance warning system.

MISCELLANEOUS

The odds and ends you will need for your backcountry foray include year-round staples, gear which will change with the changing seasons, and special-purpose equipment for specific sporting objectives. This special equipment—fishing, hunting, and photo tackle—will be dealt with in detail in chapters 5, 6, 7, and 8, but here is an annotated list of things you will always need.

Knife

Hunters will probably want a special-purpose gutting and skinning knife but everybody going into the backcountry should carry a multiple-purpose knife for trail and camp tasks.

The most celebrated and perhaps the best all-around back-packing knives are the Swiss Army knives. Only two factories in Switzerland make them, Wenger and Victorinex. Both firms make them in a variety of shapes, sizes, functions, and prices,

Knives

Any folding blade knife will do for backcountry tripping but some do much better than others. Here are three excellent varieties that will give you the edge. At left is the Wenger Swiss Army Setter with twenty-one different functions from cutting to cleaning your nails. In the middle is the Puma Universal, a hunting knife with a lock-blade main blade, a special gutting blade, a bone saw, a leather awl, and a bird gutting hook. On the right is one of the many modestly priced simple lock-blades. This one is an Explorer ZZ by Edgemark.

starting at about $15 for simple camping knives to about $40 for knives that can do just about anything but wash dishes. I use a compact, multiblade job by Wenger called the Setter.

As nice as Swiss Army knives are, they are not an absolute necessity. Any folding knife with one blade at least three inches long will do, and a lot of experienced backcountry sportsmen prefer the security of one of the numerous lock-blade folders available today. The lock blades range in price from $5 for a perfectly good single-blade import to $50 for a German-made Puma.

Sheath knives have advantages but compatibility with belts on backpacks is not one of them. Folding knives work much better.

Compass

There are people who have enough built-in direction-finding equipment to find their way out of a mangrove swamp on a moonless night. I am not one of them and neither are most people. Unless you are thoroughly familiar with your hiking territory, you would be well advised to always carry a compass and be familiar with its use. In the next chapter we will look into a few of the marvelous things a compass can do, but let's take a look at the state of the art of the instrument now.

Almost everyone has a compass of some kind, either an old Boy Scout, Army surplus, or the pin-on hunter's style. And nearly everyone knows these compasses will indicate which direction is north. Most compasses are also marked along the edge with degrees, 360 of them divided into quarters for the cardinal points.

These compasses will do to get you pointed on the right heading and, if you are a clever mathematician, you might even be able to make some basic routing computations. But there is another sytle of backpacker's compass that simplifies map orientation and route calculation so much that it is well worth the $5 to $20 that it costs. This is the clear lucite-backed azimuth orienteering compass which comes in several models. The two best are the U.S.-made Silva and the Finnish-made Suunto. I use a Suunto AR-69 DE with a built-in pace counter and declination adjustment.

First Aid Kit

The standard first aid kit should be packaged to meet health problems which might reasonably be expected in the back-country. These problems will vary from season to season, area to area, and from one sporting quest to another. The basic kit should contain: gauze tape, gauze pads, adhesive tape, bandages, soap, disinfectant, and a mild pain suppressant like aspirin. In the summer, in many areas, it should also contain a snakebite kit and during hunting season several large compress bandages.

Nearly as important as a well-stocked kit is the ability to use it, and for this a small first aid book may mean the difference between life and death. There are several such books available today, including a number of pamphlets from the Red Cross. You can either assemble your own kit in a watertight container (plastic freezing jars with tape-lapped lids work fine) or buy a ready-made package from most backpacking outfitters.

Survival Kit

A good, tight, well-stocked survival kit might be the most important piece of gear you carry into the backcountry. It is possible, however, to make this kit too big. Most commercial survival packages are big, bulky, and heavy, containing a number of things you already have in your pack.

My kit contains only enough to supplement what is already in my pack to get me through a day or two in an emergency. I have carried it for seventeen years and thousands of miles and have, so far, opened it only to see if anything has rotted. It contains two Baker's four-ounce chocolate bars, a Thermos mylar emergency space blanket, multiple vitamins, two boxes of waterproofed matches (bound in a zip lock bag), and a tube of five G.I. firestarters. The kit weighs less than a pound and, wrapped and taped into an airtight plastic bag and nylon sack, takes up less space than my traveling tobacco pouch.

Other Essentials

There are a number of things you will have to carry but they are so obvious I am embarrassed to mention them.

The first of these is a rope. Hunters will be carrying a drag rope anyway but everybody traveling in the backcountry, especially in the mountains, should have a long length of amply strong rope or cord. In the mountains you should have at least 100 feet of rope strong enough to hold your dead weight; this means a breaking strength of about 1,600 pounds to be safe. In the lowlands, fifty feet of one-eighth-inch nylon cord will do.

A simple fire bag will come in handy more often than you might think. It will not only get wet, stubborn wood blazing but is also handy when you are simply too tired to go to the bother of shaving up kindling. It consists of a waterproofed pouch of book matches and a tube of G.I. firestarters.

We have already talked about a good winter cap, but in the summer a lightweight brimmed hat can add a lot to the comfort of a hike.

Toilet tissue is necessary not only for the obvious reasons but also for use as burnable rags. Bring more than you think you will need.

In the same vein, a bandanna and a spare should be standard equipment. Besides being good for nose blowing, they are handy as emergency tourniquets, bandages, rags, markers, or flags. They also look dashing around your neck while they protect you from sunburn or around your head, where they mop up sweat.

You will also need extra clothing to make you decent and comfortable if the togs you are wearing get wet or damaged.

Sunglasses and sunburn cream will take the edge off the sun during summer days, while mosquito dope will protect you at night. Also at night, most people will need a flashlight, especially during the hunting season.

There are, no doubt, any number of things a lot of people feel are indispensable in the backcountry that are not included on this list. Baggy toilets, pillows, cast iron frying pans, and a teddy bear may be hauled faithfully up and down the trail by some, but the equipment suggested in this chapter constitutes the necessities for comfort and safety during a few days in the backcountry. With one exception, anything else is either luxury or fluff and should be measured as such before stuffing it into your already bulging pack.

This exception is an Ensolite or other closed-cell foam pad. Any strip of closed-cell foam will serve the same purpose: supplementing the loft of your sleeping bag, which, compressed by the weight of your body, provides only minimal insulation from the cold ground. An earlier answer to sleeping comfort, the air mattress, may protect you from the pebble you failed to notice when you spread the sleeping bag but is virtually useless against the cold.

MULTIPURPOSE GEAR

A backpack, like a space ship, is limited in the amount of volume and weight that can be packed aboard. Everything that goes into it must be carefully thought out and weighed to be sure it will be worth its weight. Much of the survival equipment aboard a space vehicle has more than one function, and the people who occupy space crafts must know how to get the most out of everything that is packed aboard.

The same principle applies to a well-thought out backpack; nearly everything in it can be used for more than one purpose. An obvious example is the rope, which can not only be used to help string up a tent or tarp on rocky or soft ground that won't hold a stake, but can also be used for: (1) light mountaineering tasks such as hauling packs or roping in members of a party over treacherous footing, (2) devising emergency litters and other equipment for casualties from saplings, (3) a safety rope for river or frozen lake crossings, or (4) roping in precarious emergency bivouacs.

Other equipment which has more specific purposes can also be adapted to cope with both emergency and more mundane situations. The tent fly, the waterproof roof covering, can be used alone as shelter in an awkward bivouac, a cover for an emergency litter, a waterproof ground cloth, or, tucked into a hole, a wash basin or bathtub. Your poncho raingear will do anything the tent fly will do as well as add an additional waterproof shelter to your camp for protecting gear or keeping dinner dry.

Two or more sleeping bags can be used in conjunction as quilts to protect an accident victim both in camp and on a litter. Your down vest or jacket can be stuffed into a bag to make a cozy pillow (I like to put a wool sweater or shirt over the nylon bag to add warmth and reduce the clammy feeling one gets from condensed moisture on a slick surface). Your pack itself can earn its keep in camp as a waterproof cover, a food bag suspended between two trees (yet another use for rope), or a foot sack to keep the bottom of your sleeping bag dry in a bivouac. Your Ensolite or open-cell sleeping pad is, of course, a soft seat whenever you need one, can be rigged into an emergency litter, and can insulate stoves from cold ground or snow to help keep the pressure up in the fuel tank (cold air and direct contact with a cold surface dissipates pressurized fuels).

The point, of course, is to get the very most out of everything you haul into the backcountry. Virtually every piece of gear you carry can be used for more than one function (except first aid kits and food). All that is required is a need and the ingenuity to fill it. Think of the things in your pack as a Yankee thought of his axe or a Depression-era farmer his baling wire and something can be jury-rigged to meet just about any need.

With the equipment described, your pack will probably weigh from twenty to thirty pounds, depending on the care and money you spent selecting your gear. Any less and you have probably left out something essential; any more and you will spend your backcountry time staggering under the burden of pack and sporting gear combined.

One of the most gratifying things about backcountry hiking is the knowledge that the weight on your back means that you are comfortably supporting the equipment that will comfortably support you during your days in the backcountry. Soon the things in your pack will become as familiar to you as the accessories you carry in your pocket. Each will have a feel and a heft you can recognize without seeing it. You will develop a sequence of packing which will both meld the pack with your back and place things you use often where you need them when you need them.

Everything in your pack earns its place. As you find things you thought irreplaceable still unused, they will be discarded. The longer you hike, the lighter you pack will become.

CHAPTER 2

The ABC's of Hiking

Backcountry travel is almost like flying off into space. You are leaving the comfortable security of a planned and controlled environment to explore a strange and alien place, full of new sights and sensations, where you and the few things you brought with you are on your own.

An astronaut has a space vehicle which must be designed to carry the equipment necessary for space travel, the power to escape earth's atmosphere, and the fuel to get the traveler to his destination and back. The backcountry traveler must also carefully prepare his vehicle—i.e., his legs and back—to carry himself and his gear out of the world of known quantities and condition this vehicle to deal with the stresses and unknown quantities of the backcountry.

CONDITIONING

Getting from point A to point B and back is only half the trip in the backcountry. On top of this, your body must be prepared to carry the weight that thousands of machines carry for you in the civilized world. Your muscles must perform the everyday mundane tasks such as hauling water, gathering wood (if you build a fire), and disposing of your body wastes. These same muscles must withstand the extraordinary stresses of locating, dragging, and dressing your backcountry quarry.

The latter activities alone make so many demands on pampered bodies and organs that poor conditioning is responsible for many more hunting season fatalities than shooting accidents.

There is only one way to protect your body in the backcountry and that is to temper it to the rigors it will be exposed to before you leave for the wilds. This does not mean you are going to have to go into rigid training for a month prior to your outing. On the contrary, maintaining a level of adequate conditioning is far better than a last-minute Mr. America crash course.

Making your body do the work of convenience machines is probably the best and most appropriate way of getting into shape for backcountry outings. Walk whenever it is practical rather than drive—to the store, from the train, to lunch or dinner. Use stairs instead of elevators and ramps rather than escalators. Americans travel enormous distances every day, much more than any other people in the world. If we used our legs for just a fraction of this daily distance, we would probably be among the fittest people in the world.

Jogging is probably the best way of quickly trimming up your body. However, many people find jogging not only a strain but also something of a bore. Others find, in the rhythm between ground and body, a transcendental experience which becomes an end in itself.

I happen to look at jogging as a simple tool—a quick way of hardening flabby flesh after a winter of sloth. I begin jogging in the early spring when the snow has left the valley floor and vernal vegetation has not yet poked out to test the weather. I tend to be goal-oriented (as I think most Americans are) and haven't been able to discover the metaphysical ecstasy of sore legs and short breath. I have to assign myself a difficult but attainable goal such as running a mile and a half course in twelve minutes. I know I can do it because I have done it just about every year since college, but I also know it won't be easy because the rest of my body would just as soon be sitting at home reading a book.

So I begin slowly, not even running the full course at first if the flesh rebels. After a week of conscientious ordeal, the maiden stiffness in the running gear is gone and I can pace out the distance without much trouble. By the end of the second week I have run the course in a dozen minutes a few times and feel like a four-day jaunt in the mountains.

Because I don't really like to jog, I prefer to maintain conditioning in other ways. I live in the foothills of Montana's Mission Mountains; so getting into them regularly is not much problem for me. However, most people don't have the opportunity to go backcountry tramping whenever they feel the urge; so they will need other means to maintain the edge on their body.

Tennis, or other fast-moving competitive sports, will hone this edge nearly as quickly as jogging and add that critical will to excel that most of us find so necessary to maintain enthusiasm. A good, hard three-set match can put five or six miles on your legs and provide the competitive interest to keep coming back. Tennis has other advantages over jogging as a conditioner; it forces your mind to work quickly under stress, which can be critical in the backcountry, and gives you a variety of pace, from rest stops to short, hard sprints. It also brings your arms into action and develops a keen perception of distance and direction.

Diet and general health habits are also important in preparing for a backcountry trip. Smoking is not only bad for you in the long run but also makes it difficult for your body to become and stay fit. The same can be said for even modestly excessive drinking.

A good, sound, balanced diet is as important before you leave as it is on the backcountry trail. The body needs proper food to develop and no amount of exercise is going to help if you are not getting adequate supplies of all nutritional requirements. And, of course, if you are not eating properly, you are not going to feel like exercising a great deal.

Most nutritionists agree the normal heavy evening meal is silly; carbohydrates that are not needed for energy in the evening and during the night are just going to turn to fat. A wiser course is to eat a stout, well-thought out breakfast and an ample lunch with just a snack for dinner. This way carbohydrates and protein will be able to go to work for your body during the day when they are needed, and the evening snack can see you through the night.

These are just suggestions. There are no doubt thousands of other ways of getting your body into condition which will work as well or better. The thing to remember, however, is that, like a spaceship, you are going to have to rely on your body systems for the duration of your backcountry travels. There are no telephones back there to call for a cab, and the doctor is out, way out. You and your companions will have to deal with both the ordinary and any emergencies that might arise. The comfort and safety of everyone rides on the ability of your body to function smoothly.

DIRECTION-FINDING WITH MAP AND COMPASS

Our metaphorical spaceship also has complicated navigational equipment to point it on course and keep it there. Built-in computers have cybernetic as well as discretionary functions to recognize the options and make the right choices. The backcountry wanderer should have simpler versions of this equipment.

To begin with, he must know where he is going (if not exactly at least approximately) and how to get there. U.S. Geological Service topographical (or topo) maps are the best down-to-earth way of backcountry trip planning. Topos are two-dimensional flat pieces of paper which symbolically represent the three dimensions of a given land area. The symbol used to convey the altitude of hills and valleys is the gradient line, which, when combined with other gradient lines on a topo map, shows not only the maximum or minimum elevation of a geological feature but also the varying degrees of pitch or steepness the feature will present the hiker.

Gradient lines represent intervals of either 20 or 80 feet, depending on whether the maps are 7.5-minute scale or 15-minute scale. The more intricately detailed 7.5-minute topo maps have the advantage of providing more data about slope pitches and the configuration of the surrounding topography. The 80-foot interval 15-minute maps, however, represent twice as much territory on one map, usually about 18 miles by 12 miles, minimizing the need for several maps to chart out an extended trip.

Topo maps are often available at local sporting goods stores or cartography shops or by writing Distribution Center, U.S. Geological Survey, 1200 Eads Street, Arlington, Virginia 22202; or Distribution Center, U.S. Geological Survey, Federal Center, Building 41, Denver, Colorado 80225. The maps cost from $1.00 to $1.50 depending on where you buy them.

Topo maps show, in essence, a bird's-eye view of the land. They will show you where to expect marshes, lakes, streams, and existing trails as well as the inclination of hills, mountains, and valleys. In order to put this information to practical use on the trail, you must be able to coordinate your map with a compass. With a topo map, a good compass, and a little understanding of their relationship, there is practically no such thing as being lost in the backcountry.

Although any compass with a revolving magnetized needle will show you which direction is north (and consequently the other three primary directions), most compasses are difficult or impossible to coordinate with maps. Compasses designed to complement maps are known as orienteering azimuth instruments. Normally, they are transparent-based compass housings mounted on flat, clear plastic bases.

The needle housing is filled with clear liquid in better models and marked in degrees around the face. The liquid both dampens the action of the needle and protects the delicate housing from shocks and jolts. The degrees divide the circle of the needle housing into 360 direction points. Some of the better models also include another clear plastic disc below the degree housing providing a nonmagnetic directional arrow and left and right declination markings to compensate for the difference between magnetic north and map north.

The rectangular plastic base varies in length from about three to five inches, the longer the better. The edges are normally marked with inches on one side and millimeters on the other. Many have built-in magnifying lenses to assist in reading the fine print on maps.

Better orienteering compasses, made by Suunto and Silva, are remarkably accurate and, with a little bit of simple math, can nor-

Compass and Topographical Map

These are the instruments necessary to interpret backcountry signposts.

mally pinpoint your exact location on your topo map. The only situations that make orienteering difficult are heavy overcast that obscures surrounding landmarks and featureless country such as broad marshes and swamps.

Coordinating map and compass to find out where you are is merely a matter of orienting landmarks and making calculations. To orient map to compass, spread the map out on the ground, lay the compass down on the true north location arrow on the map, and turn the map until the directional arrow of the compass, the needle, and the true north arrow on the map are all pointed in the same direction. The map is now north- or zero-oriented.

Now look around you and find a predominant landmark to the right. Let's say there is a rock protrusion from a hill over there which, you will notice on your map, is called Pat's Knob. Leaving the map in its north-oriented position, pick up the compass and rotate the directional lines on its base or an edge toward the pinnacle of Pat's Knob. When it is lined up, note the direction in degrees of the magnetic needle, which will give you your bearing. Let's say that when the zero-oriented compass is lined up with Pat's Knob, you get a reading of 300 degrees on the magnetic needle. Subtract 300 from 360 degrees and you arrive at a bearing of 60 degrees between you and the knob.

Now put the compass back on the zero-oriented map and place the straight edge of the compass against Pat's Knob. Move the compass back and forth, using the summit mark on the map as a hinge, until the magnetic needle points to 300 degrees. Draw a pencil line southwesterly along the straight edge of the compass for the first line of your triangulation calculation. (You will actually be back azimuthing from Pat's Knob at 240 degrees, the opposite of 60 degrees, but that really doesn't matter in determining your position.)

Now look off to your left (or westerly) and find another prominent landmark. There is a hill over there with a sharp cliff face on the east side. On your map you see this must be Lover's Leap by the meshing of grid lines on the south face. Pick up the compass and repeat the process of finding the azimuth of Pat's Knob. Let's say it reads an azimuth of 210 degrees. The back azimuth would be 30 degrees; so draw the line from Lover's Leap easterly on the map at that bearing. The point where the westerly line from Pat's Knob and the easterly line from Lover's Leap meet should be the place where you are standing.

But there is a hitch or two in this neat equation. The first and most critical is a little catch twenty-two known as declination. Declination is the difference between true north as shown on the map and the direction in which your compass's magnetic needle points. Your topo map will show you the degree in error between true and magnetic north. In northern Montana, where I live, declination is around twenty degrees. The further north you get in the northern hemisphere, the more the declination will be. Some compasses have mechanical declination adjustments; with others you will have to subtract or add the appropriate declination figure to your calculations. For instance, if the declination is twenty degrees east and you are sighting in on a landmark which reads sixty degrees, you should subtract twenty degrees to arrive at an adjusted figure of forty degrees. Conversely, an azimuth taken to the west (higher than 180 degrees) would show that magnetic line plus 20 degrees. If the line were 350 degrees, the actual azimuth would be 10 degrees east.

Another problem with hand-held compass orienteering is the amplification of slight errors in sighting or calculation. Depending on how much distance your triangulation process involves, an error of as little as one degree can amount to hundreds of feet in bearings by the time the line gets back to your locations on the map. Multiply this by two for an error on the second landmark and you could be off by quite some distance in your calculation. The point is be as careful as possible orienting the map and taking azimuths on landmarks, and assume a certain amount of error. If the landmarks are only a mile away the error won't amount to more than a few feet. If they are farther, you may not even be in the neighborhood but you will have a ball park estimation of your location to work with.

Spaceships are very careful with their navigational equipment because without it they would just be another piece of wandering flotsam riveted to a circular course forever. Anybody going into the backcountry should be equally careful about his map and compass for precisely the same reason. Without them you will be doomed to a course of directionless circles until it doesn't matter anymore.

Compasses should be either well attached to the body or clothing or snuggled away in a safe but easily accessible part of the pack. They should also be protected either by a case or at least a waterproof bag, and everybody in the party should carry one in case one is lost or broken.

Topo maps are made out of paper and paper, as everybody knows, is subject to all manner of wear and tear. Maps may be totally destroyed by fire or drenching or lose fidelity through wear in the corners and in the creases. Many experienced backpackers sheathe their maps between sheets of self-adhering plastic laminates. This process costs about $1.25 per map. Others cut their maps along the folding seams and glue the pieces in sequence to a piece of cloth, preferably lightweight nylon. Most nylons cost at least $3 per yard, which is enough for two maps, or $1.50 per map. Considering the price of topo maps and their virtual pricelessness in the backcountry, either method would probably be a good investment. If these ounces of prevention seem excessive, at least put your maps in a water-resistant plastic bag (the zip lock food bags are ideal) and carry it in a safe place in your pack.

THE DEMANDS OF HIKING

Hiking with thirty to forty-five extra pounds on your back is to strolling down a street about as formula racing is to highway driving. The motions and mechanics are about the same, but the amount of concentration required is greatly increased and the margin for error is commensurately reduced. When out for a spin in the family car, you can afford to divert some attention to the radio, the scenery, or to day-dreaming; conditioning and reflexes will do most of the driving for you and give you enough response time to deal with the unexpected. A race car driver, however, does not have this margin of safety and cannot afford to allow attention to lapse. He must anticipate everything that will or might happen because, at 150 miles per hour, his reflexes won't be fast enough to react to a sudden situation. Driving is his only business and he is continually on the naked edge of winning or death.

Backpacking differs from a leisurely stroll in about the same way and to the same degree. When walking down a sidewalk your legs are carrying only your normal weight along an even and predictable surface. You can afford to gaze at passers-by, gawk into store windows, think about pleasant things or hopscotch if you feel like it. If you should stumble on an exposed crack, your body has sufficient muscular and neurological reflexes to maintain your equilibrium. Even if you should fall and twist an ankle or bang a knee, help is not far away and all you will suffer is a lot of embarrassment and a little pain.

But under load in the backcountry, walking is nearly as demanding a pursuit as race car driving. That is why the language has separated the casual function of walking from the more intense occupation of hiking or backpacking. With a load on your back, every step on an uneven and often dangerous trail is critical. A slight depression in the trail can throw you off balance enough so the weight of your pack will overcome your body's ability to recover; down you go with a third again as much weight-generated force as you would normally have to sustain. A loose rock on a thin mountain trail can exponentially multiply this extra thirty to forty-five pounds into a savage tumble down an embankment. Mountain climbers never move either their feet or their hands without knowing exactly what the change in hold will mean. A backpacker should be equally cautious about where his feet will fall while keeping another eye on branches, fallen logs, or jutting rocks that could garrot, trip, or knock him off balance.

This does not mean that hiking with a pack on your back is a matter of stopping after every step to carefully measure the terrain in front of you, but it does mean you have to set a hiking stride that allows you to keep wind and head, consciously observe trail obstacles, and make the appropriate adjustments. On most trails this will not usually entail breaking stride but off trail, where grass and forest debris can conceal pitfalls, hiking rhythm may have to operate at two or more speeds.

RHYTHM

Rhythm in hiking is the timing and sequence of putting one foot in front of the other. The rhythm of a hike is affected by several considerations: (1) the difficulty or pitch of the terrain or trail, (2) the distance to be covered during the day's hike, (3) the physical abilities of the slowest member of the party, and (4) the reason you are out in the boondocks hiking in the first place.

This latter consideration we will deal with in detail in chapter 6. To give you fair warning ahead of time, it means adjusting the hiking rhythm to something akin to what the old submarine movies called quiet running—stalking or still-hunting with pack to enhance the chances of seeing game.

A hiking party, to use yet another tired simile, is like a convoy of ships; it can only move as fast as its slowest member. This means every member in the party should be about physically equal. If not, there is a tendency to allow slower members to string out behind (a discourteous and unsafe practice), or the faster members will become bored. Nonetheless, if there is a variation in speed of the members of the party, the group should try to hold together without unduly tiring anyone.

REST STOPS

Hiking is not a matter of continual trudge, one foot in front of the other until an objective is reached. Even soldiers on forced march take ten once in a while. A hiker or hiking party should fig- ure in plenty of tens, twenties, and even thirties as part of any backcountry itinerary. If you can't moon over the view, an inter- esting tree or plant while you are on the march, you are going to have to stop to do it. A sweltering military pace may reach a des- tination more quickly; but the noise, stumbling, and panting is going to clear the area of wildlife.

Frequent brief stops, at least every half hour, with longer snack stops every couple of hours, will keep everyone alert, rested, and happily hiking.

FOOD FOR THE TRAIL

Snack stops are not only a good chance to catch a breath and a good look at the country, but also a pleasant way of replenishing burned-up body fuel. Rarely in everyday life do Americans actually consume more energy than they eat. In the sedentary world carbohydrates and fats are normally run through the system without being burned or are stored in accumulating layers of fat. In the backcountry, where muscle cells are under constant stress, the body needs a constant replenishment of these quick-energy foods.

Candy bars and fruits will do but their nutritional value is limited. A better-balanced and more wholesome trail food is a mixture of nuts, fruits, cereal, and sugars known as "gorp." Gorp stands for "Good Old Reliable Peanuts" but can contain peanuts and just about anything else. Purists mix nearly equal portions of dried fruits and nuts in a plastic bag and virtually live on this for the duration of the trip. Most people add a handful of chocolate candies and another equal portion of granola cereal, packing enough to get them through trail snack stops, breakfasts, and lunches.

Although gorp is normally eaten dry, I carry a one-quart envelope of fat-added dry milk in my snack bag and occasionally mix gorp and milk. It adds both variety and protein.

I also carry a bag of instant lemonade in my snack pack. The junk food artificial kind is mostly sugar and will recharge sagging batteries at a streamside stop.

CALCULATING THE TIME REQUIRED FOR A HIKE

The time it takes a hiker to reach a destination is related to his hiking pace. Pace is affected by all the factors which determine the amount of country that can be hiked in a given amount of time. It takes into account: (1) the experience of the hikers, (2) the difficulty of the trail, (3) the weight being carried in packs, (4) the rhythm of the hike, (5) the number of stops anticipated, and, of course, (6) the amount of distance that must be covered. The pace is naturally going to be easier for an all-day five-mile hike than for a ten-mile trek.

It takes a good analytical eye and a lot of experience to be able to predict accurately how much distance a party can cover over a given course in a given amount of time. Maps will tell you precisely how many climbs you will encounter on your route, and how steep and long they will be. They will give you a good idea of obstacles you can expect.

For instance, tightly packed elevation lines on your map over the route you intend to travel indicate a sharp climb. A solid blue line shows the presence of a year-around running steam, while a blue-outlined circle designates a lake. A blue patch of tufts represents a marsh or swamp. All of these things will take time to circumvent and that extra time will have to be added to other factors in determining pace.

It is hard to generalize about the pace a group can expect to maintain because there are so many variables. A group that is not accustomed to hiking should probably allow for a pace of a little less than a mile per hour on a fairly level trail. This means the group should plan a slow hiking day to reach an objective eight miles away. I would add an hour for good measure and, of course, another hour or so to set up camp and enjoy camp activities.

Now we are talking about ten or eleven hours of sunlight for an eight-mile hike. If you are taking an off-trail route, better double the amount of time allotted. The same amount of time may be needed to hike four miles.

Now let's add pitch to the formula. On well-kept trails you should add about one hour for every thousand feet to be climbed (but don't subtract an hour for a thousand feet of descent) and two hours for every thousand off the trail. Now we are talking about a 7-mile, 1,000-foot climb as a target pace for a starting party on an average summer hiking day. Off trail, depending on the difficulty of the conditions, you may have to be satisfied with only a couple of miles per day.

And remember, fall and early winter days are considerably shorter than summer days. In October there are less than twelve total hours of light; so anticipated hunting bivouacs or campsites may have to be less ambitious than fishing camps in the summer.

CHAPTER 3

Tackling Rough Terrain

Although our legs, with a few simple and common aids and a modified walking technique called hiking, are sufficient to get us into much of the fair weather backcountry, there are areas that present special terrain problems and will require special tools and skills to traverse them safely and comfortably.

These remote and foreboding places—the mountains, moors, river bottoms, and winter backcountry—are the heart of this wild phenomenon we have been talking about. They have all of the characteristics of the backcountry but they have been cut in harder, more demanding material.

These areas differ from the pathed backcountry as much as trails differ from sidewalks. Finding a way into them is often almost as difficult as actually getting there, and you will have to use your proficiency in map-reading and overland route orienteering to the utmost just to get yourself pointed in the right direction.

And the getting there is no picnic either. Not only will you need special equipment and learn how to use it and your body in different ways, you are also going to have to spend more energy in different ways to reach areas where most people wouldn't even consider going. You will be defying natural barriers which wiser common counsel would avoid.

But the rewards of the backcountry exceed the investment. The advantages the hike-in backcountry offers over more accessible recreational areas are multiplied at an exponential rate as the difficulty of the terrain increases. The wariness of backcountry quarry—fish, mammals, and birds—evaporates into innocent curiosity as you travel farther off the beaten path.

Quarry learn to deal with specifically human threats by experience and contact with humans. The fewer humans a population of fish or game encounter, the less conditioning they will have and the probability of hooking or bagging them will be increased. Game beyond the trail and the tromp of most people often live entire lifetimes in blissful ignorance of the two-footed predator.

Foot trails into the backcountry, which are normally maintained by the compaction of use, usually end when most people who contribute to their making and grooming decide the difficulty of terrain ahead is not worth the effort to continue. Other trails avoid excessively difficult country by going around it on their way to another destination. Many trails are goal-directed, ending at a lake, mountain, or stream, and then looping back toward the trailhead. However, almost all foot trails began as game paths and usually show vague signs of being intersected frequently by the comings and goings of game.

FOLLOWING GAME TRAILS

Game trails are dynamic and seldom retain the same course over a period of years. That, combined with the fact that they are usually faint, often difficult, and don't lead to places most human beings would want to go, usually precludes them from maps.

But game animals don't make things any tougher on themselves than they have to, and their trails are often excellent overland routes which carry you off the beaten path and into the sitting room of nature.

Game trails are probably the easiest and most pleasant way of negotiating your way overland into the remote backcountry and, if you are big game hunting or taking pictures, undoubtedly one of the most profitable.

But just because you are on the path doesn't mean you can afford to be too casual about direction. Game trails usually splinter and branch off like a maze and it pays to take a bearing reading with your compass and map when you leave the foot trail and maintain your bearings while working the game trails. Another way to keep tabs on your route is to mark it occasionally with stacked stones or sticks stuck in the ground. This can prevent your becoming sidetracked on your way back.

You will probably not need any extra gear for making your way along a game trail but you can expect to find some difficult footing. What presents a casual stride to a mule deer can be a fairly difficult pitch to an off-trail hiker with a pack on his back. Wading a two-foot-deep stream may be an everyday thing to a marsh whitetail deer, but to a hiker it can present a difficult problem, especially in the fall or winter when the water is cold.

Most game animals, especially deer, never get farther away from a source of water than they have to. This means you will probably have sufficient water available during your game trail hike, but it is wise to hedge by taking along ample reserves in canteens.

The propensity of game for water can also pay off for off-trail fishermen. Game paths can lead to some pretty remarkable ponds and lakes with healthy populations of dumb fish.

One bleak fall day several years ago, a friend and I began hitching up a thinly visible game path in the Iron Country of Michigan's Upper Peninsula. The trail started in rolling hillocks but after about three miles of easy hoofing we descended into what seemed like an endless and featureless marsh (except for a thick and even blanket of briers and brambles). The next three miles was a matter of alternately crawling through brush tunnels and over fallen logs and hopping streams and bogs. Suddenly the cover melted away into a broad opening of quaking marl and hummocks graced in the middle with an ancient beaver pond.

Both of us fished the area regularly and thought we knew every nook of trout water but neither of us had even heard hints that such a Nirvana existed (of course in Upper Michigan, a beaver pond in the middle of nowhere was as valuable as a Swiss bank account and nobody in his right mind would reveal its location to his mother).

We dug the map out of my pack and checked the area for the pond. Nothing. The marsh was there but on the map it was unrelieved for miles, just a mass of tiny blue tussocks.

We walked around the pond carefully, looking simultaneously for deer along the fringes, trout along the shore, and signs of human activity. It was apparent from the criss-crossed trails that game used the pond routinely. There were some vivid-colored trout mulling along the banks and, we agreed with relief, no tell-tale people litter.

We bivouacked along the edge of the clearing on firm ground next to one of the feeder burns and slept soundly that night dreaming of leaping trout and rising mayflies.

My chum nudged me awake at the glimmer of dawn as he sat up and reached for his rifle. Not thirty yards away at the edge of the pond stood a young, healthy four-point buck trying to decipher some message in the wind from the other end of the pond. He died quickly and cleanly. The shot started a veritable stampede around the pond, which didn't matter because one animal would be enough to carry out of the thorny jungle behind us. And it was. It took us the entire day to carry, haul, and drag him through our lightly cut return trail. That night we had to bivouac again above the edge of the marsh where, as lucky streaks will often have it, I too got a decent two-year-old buck.

To make a fish story short, we returned to the pond nearly every week during the next fishing season, carefully making sure we weren't followed and varying our entry points to avoid blazing a trail. We did well there, never anything sensational but always enough to brighten our evening meal. What we couldn't eat, we returned and my chum, who still lives there, continues to fish on the interest of our discovery without touching the principal.

MOUNTAIN TRAVEL

Mountains and hills comprise more of the landscape of the United States than you might think. Mountain ranges virtually dominate the horizons west of the Continental Divide and there are few places in the north-south line between South Dakota and Texas which are not within a couple hours' drive of the mountains.

The Appalachians which cut inland along the eastern seaboard provide numerous mountain chains from Maine to Alabama. Even in the relatively flat Midwest and great plains there are countless pockets of mountains and hills from Michigan's Hurons in the north to the Ozarks and Arkansas in the south. Virtually every major river system rises from drainage hills and creates its own hill ranges on its way to the sea.

The point is, you don't have to travel to the Rockies to be in the mountains; just look around you. No matter where you live you will find some high country.

Backcountry trips involving a mountain, whether it is a 600-foot pinnacle on the Keweenaw Peninsula or a 14,000-foot peak in the Olympics, should be well planned in advance. Even if you don't intend to go to the top (there are, after all, few lakes and even fewer game animals on the peaks of most mountains), you will still be dealing with starker, steeper terrain which makes falling easier and falls much harder. The likelihood of disabling accidents in the mountains is much higher than on level trails. Careful route planning and orientation can greatly reduce the hazards of the mountains by giving you an accurate idea of the easiest route and what to look for.

One of the more demanding aspects of mountain travel is the absolute need to know exacty where you are at all times. Being a "little lost" on flat country is no big deal; just get out your compass and map and find yourself again. In the mountains being ten or fifteen feet from where you should be can be a matter of life or death.

The reason mountain routes must be maintained so religiously is a climbing law which seems to fly in the face of Newtonian physics. Whoever climbs up does so much easier than he will climb down. When you are ascending a pitch, your hands are working at eye level and your feet will be moving from lower holds to holds that are easily within view. Descending, however, your hands are working below the level of your eyes and your feet are actually feeling for holds without much assistance from your eyes. If you don't believe it, try walking downstairs backwards.

In the mountains you will find it a breeze working up a dead-end pitch such as a rock chimney. But when you discover you took the wrong route and the chimney peters out into a flat perpendicular surface, you will find it a different matter to get back down. Most mountaineering accidents happen when a party or individual climber strays off route and is forced to retreat.

The most serious danger of retreating on a pitch, especially for novice mountaineers, comes from the opposite reactions of "freezing" and "melting." Both are motivated by panic; one is the inability to move and the other is moving too quickly without thinking.

When I was just a wet-nosed kid from flatland Michigan, I took on my first mountain, Nez Perce in the Wyoming Tetons, which is nearly as high as Michigan is wide (well, so it seemed). We began the ascent early in the morning on the wrong foot, and that clad in tennis shoes. We didn't have a rope or other equipment or even lunch—just ourselves and our idiotic enthusiasm and the assurance that we were immortal.

My partner was a small, wiry Connecticut Yankee whose hobby back home was running up and down the Berkshires. He had climbed other Tetons before and had a vague notion of what the easiest route up Nez Perce was and how to get there.

Everything was going well until we hit the end of a thread-thin ledge. "I guess this isn't the easy route," he admitted, adding that we would have to go back down to another ledge to reconnoiter. I took one look below me and noticed the next firm foothold was a good 1,000 feet down. I decided it was time for a good, long reconnoiter right where we were.

I was, as the expression goes, "frozen," locked into the tenuous security of a thin four-point hold. I now think it was there, at the age of twenty, that I realized for the first time I was mortal. Sooner or later I would succumb to the way of all flesh, and at that time and place sooner seemed more probable than later.

Against all expectations, we got back down to the main ledge, discovered where we had gone wrong, and continued up until we reached the summit. But I have never forgotten that feeling of stark terror which resulted from running out of places to go. Since then I have never allowed myself to be led up a blind alley in the mountains. I either know where I am going or I don't go.

Although we are not talking about mountain climbing as

such—that is an entirely different matter from rambling around in the mountains and requires a whole new set of rules and skills—keeping to exact routes is critically important in all mountain travel.

Knowing where I am all the time in the mountains requires frequent map and bearing checks and an occasional triangulation to ease my mind. None of this is very difficult when you are at a level with or above most of the surrounding landmarks. Also, the contours of the slope often are quite distinct and it is easy to find your location exactly by identifying them on the map. If I am working a particularly difficult pitch which could give me trouble on the way back, I usually pencil in my ascent route on my map so I will have something to follow on the return leg.

Since we are not talking about mountain climbing, special technical mountaineering equipment should not be needed. However, since we are moving around in steep terrain, some generalized mountaineering gear is necessary and some special-purpose tools often pay for their weight.

The Uses of Rope

The first piece of generalized mountaineering gear you will need is a good, long stout rope. Actually, I feel that ropes are so basic to backcountry travel that I consider them standard equipment no matter where I go. If I don't anticipate steep exposure, I am content with 100 feet of ¼-inch braided nylon. These ropes normally have a stated breaking strength of 1,600 pounds (I take that with a grain of salt), which will support your climbing or skidding weight and possibly your dead weight but not your falling weight.

When I know I am going to be in areas with more exposure, I carry ⁵⁄₁₆-inch goldline rope about 150 feet long. These ropes have an actual breaking strength of about 3,000 pounds, hold knots better than nylon, and provide enough surface friction for handholds whenever they are needed.

In steep country I also carry along an additional length of one-quarter-inch braided nylon rope which is often handier than the longer, heavier goldline and can be cut into pieces for special uses.

The most common use of a rope on steep slopes is as a security line connecting members of the party. Theoretically, if one member slips in a connected team the rest should be able to arrest the fall before he is hurt or the others are pulled down too. And this is almost always the case. Among mountain climbers, falls are relatively common but almost everybody lives to tell about them because other members of the rope team know how to prepare for the fall and how to react to it when it does occur.

On a steep pitch where a fall becomes a possibility, only one member of the rope team moves at any given time. The others, which may be one or more, are firmly established in a position where they can break the fall with the rope. This position is known as a belay and it requires the consideration of a number of factors.

In the first place it must be strong enough to prevent the belayer from being pulled down. This requires finding a position where the belayer has enough room to use his weight against the pull of a fall, preferably a position with strong enough projections to tie him into the spot. Tieing in should never be done with the climbing rope, because the friction of a running rope against a stone projection would probably sever it. Rather, this is one of the places the lighter, one-quarter-inch nylon braid comes in handy. The belayer should tie himself in as high as possible, preferably around the chest so the pull of the fall won't throw him off balance. His belay point, however, should be as low as possible to give him more leverage against the pull of the fall. The best way to accomplish this is to sit with your back away from the direction of the pull with your chest tied into a strong hold.

The second consideration of a belay is to retard the speed of the fall as much as possible before the climbing rope puts the force of the fall against its knot around the belayer's body. The longer the fall is allowed to continue without partial breaking, the greater the possibility of injury to the person who is falling. The more intense the strain on the rope, the harder it is going to be to belay.

The belayer must always have control of the excess rope between himself and the climber. The belayer coils this slack beside him, feeding line to the climber as it is needed. If the climber begins to fall, the belayer gathers in as much slack as possible and, if conditions permit, continues to pull the falling climber toward him. Needless to say, both hands should be on the rope at all times and the hands should be gloved.

If there is a third person on the rope, he too should take a strong position during the belay for the first climber. When the first climber reaches the end of the pitch, the third person moves up to the second person's position. The second person then climbs up the pitch belayed both by the lead climber above and the third person below. The third person is then belayed from above by the first two as he works up the pitch.

Belays and even rope-ins should be very rare during back-country overland sporting jaunts. Even the remotest of alpine lakes are usually accessible without going to a lot of bother and worry, and most big game species would prefer not to scramble unless they are pushed. But some people are less able to deal with heights and exposure, and even a relatively easy pitch can bring on fits of acrophobia. If somebody is having a difficult time, haul out the rope. They will feel better and perform better, and an ounce of caution does have its value, especially in the backcountry.

Ropes can also help you out of tight situations in the mountains and hills. They can, for instance, make getting down from those blind alleys we talked about earlier less traumatic and much safer. In big-time mountaineering coming down a rope is known as "rappelling," a process of literally skidding down the rope using your body as a friction lever. Mountain climbers use the rappel not only to get themselves out of tight spots but also to speed up the descent from a mountain. However, rappelling requires a heavier rope (because it will have to sustain the full dead pull of a falling body) and a lot of skill. Our use of the rope will be restricted to providing ample security while we climb down the same way we came up.

As with a belay, the security rope should never be attached directly to the anchor, which can be a rock projection, a well-rooted tree, or maybe some special equipment we will talk about later, both for the same reason and the fact you will want to retrieve your rope. Rather, the anchor should be secured to a loop or doubled loop of your one-quarter-inch nylon utility rope and the security rope looped through it with the ends tied. This means a 150-foot climbing rope will shrink to a 75-foot doubled security rope. If the pitch is more than the length of your doubled rope, you will have to anchor another loop when you hit the bottom of the first length.

The climbing rope can be retrieved by untying the knot at the bottom and slipping it back by pulling on one free end. The loop rope, however, will remain where it is until somebody else picks it up; this is one of the negative trade-offs of mountaineering—the amount of gear left in and around mountains after a party has left.

The basic knot of mountaineering is the bowline (see illustration), which is used for just about everything from tying in the climbing rope to attaching slings. The venerable old Boy Scout square knot is a good way of connecting sling loops, provided you knot the ends first to prevent it from slipping.

A long, stout rope is also standard equipment for mountain big game hunting. More often than not, hoisting a dead animal down steep slopes is the only way of getting it down. Dragging or carrying simply won't work over steep terrain.

Boots

Although lightweight trail boots work fine in the flat country, in the mountains your feet and ankles are subject to abuses from all directions and you will need a stiffer, heavier boot. Boots are normally classified as light, medium, and heavy. Lightweights save weight and cost by using thinner leather, attaching the uppers directly to the Vibram soles, and paring down ankle padding. The emphasis is on flexibility and weight to make long miles on an easy trail not so tiring.

Heavyweights, which weigh over five pounds a pair, can be divided into two subgroups: mountaineering boots and expedition boots. Mountaineering boots are beefed up hiking boots made of heavy leather with strong ankle support and several layers of innersole between the uppers and Vibram. Expedition boots are made for the extemely severe conditions of winter alpine mountaineering and usually consist of a massive boot with an integral inner shoe.

Another specialized mountaineering boot is the Kletter, a technical rock climbing shoe. This is actually a lightweight boot with a narrow, heavy sole.

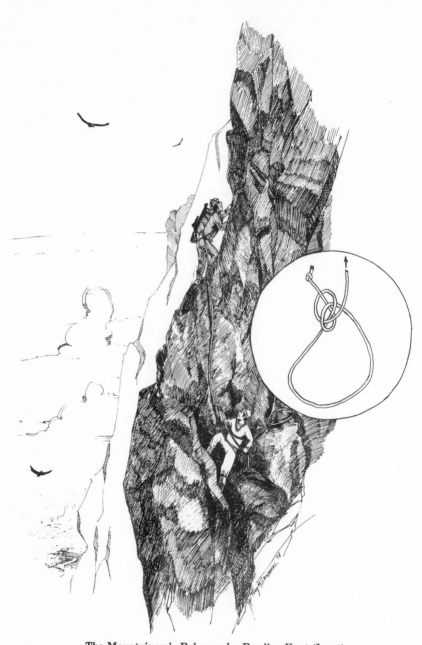

The Mountaineer's Belay and a Bowline Knot (Inset)

*The belayer ropes himself into a strong position and feeds rope to the climber.
(Drawing by Tony M. Sandoval)*

Although you can get away with one of these special-purpose heavy boots in the mountains, you don't need them. The soles on all of these boots are too thick and rigid for distance hiking and that, combined with their greater weight, will tire your feet.

The medium or light mountaineering boots are ideal for mountain or hill hiking and scrambling. They are usually much stouter than lightweights, provide ample ankle support without sacrificing flexibility, and have one inner sole to protect feet from sharp rocks. They normally weigh from four to five pounds, but there is not an ounce you will not need in the mountains.

Ice Axe

An ice axe is a marginal necessity in the mountains. I usually take one along in the late fall or winter or in other seasons if I expect to run into snowfields or glaciers. They are handy for cutting footsteps along compacted snow or icy slopes, as a walking aid and probe on snowfields, as a ground stake to bolster a belay, or as a support for general camping and bivouac purposes.

An ice axe usually has a relatively short shaft and a two-function head. One end of the head has a horizontal cutting edge, the other a serrated pick. The bottom of the shaft usually has a tempered steel point to allow it to penetrate hard crust.

Most ice axes come with or have optional carrying cords available. These are looped around your wrist so if you drop the axe on a slope it won't go far. I modified this cord so I can attach it to the head of the axe, providing a sling for carrying it over my shoulder like a rifle.

There are two disadvantages to ice axes. In the first place, they represent a couple of pounds of mostly dead weight which you may never need. Snowfields and glaciers can usually be avoided in the temperate months and there are dangers on winter slopes that an ice axe can't cope with, although I would never try to negotiate one without an axe.

The second problem is the initial cost of an ice axe. They range from $30 to $60 and, if I didn't already have one, I am not sure they represent enough value for me to buy one at that price. It is easier and cheaper to avoid situations where an ice axe is necessary.

Carabiners

Among the other anxiety equipment I usually haul into the hills are a pair of generalized mountaineering implements, carabiners and rock nuts.

Carabiners are oval or D-shaped rings about three inches long and an inch broad. They have spring-loaded or screw-locking gates along one long plane to allow snapping them to ropes, slings, or other rings.

Their chief value is in expediting rope use. Instead of tying a climbing rope around my body I make a doubled body sling out of ¼-inch nylon, tie a bowline in the climbing rope, and connect the loop to my body sling with a carabiner. This allows me to change my position on the climbing rope quickly and without a great deal of unknotting or fuss.

Carabiners also come in handy as anchors for ascending ropes. Rather than using a rope sling loop or sharp rock projection, I loop my rope through a carabiner. The carabiner is sacrificed but it saves time and makes a smoother slip for the rope when you have hit bottom.

Rock Nuts

The carabiner and another mountaineering implement called a rock nut can get you out of a tight scrape when there are no handy projections to loop a sling around. Nuts, as the name implies, are four- and six-sided blocks with a hole in the middle—as in nuts and bolts. They are usually made of aluminum, and the edges of the bearing surfaces are concentric to create a wedge effect between various top and bottom combinations. When a nut is placed in a crack in the rocks, the two bearing surfaces bind into the space, providing a secure hold. A carabiner can be snapped in and the climbing rope looped through for a descent. The carabiner and nut will probably be lost in the operation but occasionally both can be recovered by flailing the rope up, working the carabiner against the friction hold of the nut, and driving it out of the crack.

Aluminum carabiners cost about $4 each and are probably worth it if you anticipate using a rope at all. Nuts, depending on size, cost from \$3 to \$5 each and, with any luck, won't be needed. However, luck is fickle; so I always carry a couple in small and medium size to hedge my bets in the mountains.

The essentials, in the mountains, hills or ridges, are at least a 100-foot length of 1,600-pound test rope; stout, medium-weight mountain boots, and leather gloves. You won't absolutely need, but may wish you had, another 100 feet of at least the same strength rope, an ice axe, a couple of carabiners and a brace of rock nuts.

Maintaining Balance

There are a few tricks involved in using your feet and body on slopes and mountain trails. The first and most critical is to avoid the natural inclination to bend your body in the direction of the slope. Most people have the reflex of moving the top of their body away from the exposed side of a thin mountain ledge. The rationale, if there is any, may be that if one is going to fall down that thousand-foot cliff, one doesn't want to land on one's head. Actually, however, by shifting your weight from the center of your feet, you are increasing the possibility of a slip or skid toward the exposed side. You are also displacing your center of balance so if you do begin to slip, you will have a more difficult time recovering.

The trick, in the mountains as well as on the level, is to keep as much of your weight directly over your feet as possible. This is safer and less tiring because it not only gives you better balance but also requires less exertion to maintain that balance.

Another counterproductive natural tendency when going up or down inclines is to swing your legs higher than they need to go to reach the next step. The leading leg, with the body straight over it, should be moved ahead just enough to catch the next step. If you stoop into the slope, your legs will have to move farther than necessary to catch up with the forward center of gravity. Keep your body straight, your stride even and your step economical.

Poor decision-making can also be a problem in the mountains. It is easy to lose your head for a moment and make panicky decisions. If you get into a fix, relax a second, force yourself to think it over carefully, and measure the options. You don't have enough margin for error in the hills to allow for quick judgments.

TRAVEL ON SNOW

Snow presents the most common backcountry travel problem. Almost all of the United States gets a little bit every year and most of the country gets enough to require special equipment for hiking off the beaten path during the winter.

Snow presents a special problem for several reasons. The mild, easy trails of summer, spring, and fall are transformed into a difficult and sometimes treacherous element by the gentle accumulation of snow. Concomitant with snow is the cold of winter, which may not materially affect your footing but will definitely affect your comfort and well-being. These two problems, traveling on snow and protecting yourself from the cold, are the special situations which must be dealt with in the winter backcountry.

There are occasions, usually during the early spring, when the combination of top compaction and a few warm days transforms the surface of the snow into a thick, hard crust which can hold the weight of a fully equipped hiker. This phenomenon creates an immense paved walkway, making backcountry traveling faster and easier than at any other time. This smooth, white, hard floor is a gift from Nature and being out on it is one of the true joys of the backcountry. Such conditions are rare, however, subject to quick and violent change, and don't have much to do with backcountry diversions (although big game animals are usually yarded up at this time of the year and the wildlife photographer can have a field day in the dense timber stands and creek bottoms).

The soft snows of late fall and early winter are the conditions most often encountered by big game hunters; hard winter snow cover is the special terrain of the backcountry ice fisherman.

Fall snows are normally not deep enough to warrant flotation footgear such as skis or snowshoes, but late hunting in the northern tier of states almost always requires such equipment.

If popularity is any measure of worth, cross-country skis must be infinitely superior to snowshoes in all snow conditions. Cross-country skiing has erupted from a quaint way of getting around in the snowy bush to a national wintertime phenomenon.

Popularity seldom has much to do with value, however, and the snowshoe, cross-country ski trade-off might be as good an example as you can find. Skis work well in their own element, tightly consolidated powder snow firm enough to hold the skis up and with texture enough to allow some control. Tough, crust snow, soft, fluffy snow, and wet snow present frustrating problems to cross-country skiers.

Snowshoes will handle any snow equally well. Most designs offer enough flotation to keep the hiker on top of the fluffiest snow, and they will keep plodding along in slush or crust when skiers have either sunk out of sight or disappeared over a crusty ridge they couldn't navigate.

Flotation is the principle behind both skis and snowshoes. This does not mean you can walk on water with them; it means they present enough surface to the snow to distribute your body weight and keep you from sinking. A booted foot has about twenty square inches of surface. If you weigh 200 pounds, that means your pressure on the ground is about ten pounds per square inch, too much to support you under most snow conditions.

A 3-inch-wide, 7-foot-long trail ski, on the other hand, gives you about 250 square inches of surface, or a ground pressure of about .8 pound. A big trail snowshoe will give you over 750 square inches of snow-covering surface, which maths out to about .27 pound of ground pressure per inch. Obviously you are going to stay on top of the snow better with your weight so lightly distributed.

Snowshoes

If you are going to be in the backcountry at different times throughout the winter, snowshoes are probably the best way to go. The big bent hickory and rawhide trail types are not necessarily the best choice. There is a point of diminishing return on the benefits of surface area. The larger the surface, the more awkward and clumsy the shoes will be. There is an optimum ground surface size which will give you both adequate flotation and ample freedom of movement. To me, that size is about 400 to

500 square inches, or about the range of the traditional teardrop-shaped pattern known as the bearpaw.

I have been using a pair of bearpaws for about ten years and so far haven't found a snow condition they could not handle at least moderately well. These arty hickory and rawhide shoes are somewhat fragile and are getting fairly expensive (about $50). Another type of snowshoe has emerged which is probably a better value, all things considered.

The new shoes are called Sherpas and are made of aluminum frames with neoprene lacing. The larger size of these long narrow shoes has about the same flotation as the bearpaws I now use. I tried a pair a couple of times last winter and was impressed with their easy handling, especially on slopes where an optional creeper tooth bar for the bottoms opens up a whole new range of winter hiking. They are expensive, about $80, but I am convinced that when my bearpaws will paw no more, I will probably trade them in for a pair of Sherpas.

Snowshoes have the advantage of being less difficult to master than skis. Just about anybody who can walk can get around on snowshoes, although it takes practice and experience to cover long hauls without becoming fatigued.

The trick is to walk as economically and as gracefully as a pair of size ninety-nine dancing shoes will allow. Most snowshoers carry a ski pole or ice axe to help maintain balance and reduce the energy required to move them.

At first you will have to lift the front-heavy toes much higher than necessary because the nose will tend to catch in the snow. After a while, you will find that by partially lifting the front of the shoe and bringing it forward with the bottom of the toe scraping you can achieve a smooth, easy gait which won't win you any cross-country races but will get you around in the snow without turning your legs into mush.

Cross-Country Skis

Cross-country skis are like poetry to the prose of snowshoes. They require a great deal more time and skill to master, are more restricted in the type of snow they can handle, are less practical (and more expensive), more delicate, more sensitive, and require more hardware. But, once mastered and in their element, they are as graceful as a Yeats stanza, as exhilarating as a Beethoven quartet, as personal as a Kierkegaard parable, and as coolly efficient as a mathematical formula.

In the late fall and early winter when the first heavy snow is on the northern states' hunting grounds, cross-country skis can be as fast and as deadly a hunting weapon as a powerful and accurate rifle. Wax-bottomed skis move quickly through the winter landscape with a murmuring hush. A skilled skier can move as fast in these conditions as a deer and do it so quietly and with so little motion that game animals are caught with their senses down. In their time and place, well-tuned skis and a skilled skier can see and do things that most people only dream about.

There are basically three generic types of cross-country skis available: (1) the heavy, long Nordic touring skis designed for protracted winter excursions, (2) the long, slender skating cross-country ski, which is light, fine, and delicate for trail skiing, and (3) the short, fat, stubby Bushwhackers designed for off-trail ventures in mixed snow conditions.

Touring skis are made to withstand the abuse of long, tough trips in the mountains. They are heavy and hard to carry although they will last longer under any circumstances than the lighter models. Ski touring is usually a mixed bag of winter travel including skiing, hiking, and hiking and climbing assisted by crampons (special toothed harnesses for the bottoms of boots). For this reason, bindings on touring skis are usually designed to accommodate either special skiing boots or regular mountaineering hiking boots.

Trail skis, or the long, narrow cross-country variety, are probably the most popular of the breed because they are light and fast. They are made for effortless gliding along flat, even terrain. Their lightness, which is so attractive on clean trails, makes them less suitable for rough brushy country and uneven terrain. With trail skis a fallen log can be a major obstacle to cross and an unseen rock or dip can splinter the fronts of the skis, transforming them instantly into inadequate, clumsy snowshoes.

The characteristic fragility of trail skis renders them less than ideal for extended backcountry excursions. They work fine until they don't work at all; then they are worse than nothing. A broken

Snow Flotation Gear

On the left is a long, narrow cross-country ski designed for fast flatland travel. In the center is a short, stubby Bushwhacker ski which can handle rougher country than the cross-country. On the right is a venerable old hickory and rawhide trail snowshoe, one of the most reliable ways of hoofing through the snow.

tip or splintered bottom can transform an idyllic winter weekend into an ordeal or worse. There are special plastic tips which snap onto the broken end of a ski, and it is possible to tie your boot back onto a torn-out binding; but the return trip won't be the breeze-in-your-face affair getting there was.

The Bushwhacker, a relatively new and innovative style of backcountry ski, is kind of a cross between snowshoes and touring skis. It is short, about five feet long, wide (three and one-half inches), and reasonably stout. Bushwhackers don't glide as readily as trail skis but can handle a greater variety of snow conditions, are more agile around obstacles such as fallen logs, are less likely to break, and can be used like snowshoes over brushy spots. The current line of Bushwhackers have vinyl fish-scale bottoms rather than wood and are available with steel edges, which makes them more controllable by giving them a cutting edge on the snow.

Fragile trail skis are too thin and fine to take anything but shoe bindings but Bushwhackers have enough heft at the mounting platform to take full-scale touring bindings, a real advantage over their racier cousins.

The three basic types of ski cost about the same, from $150 to $200, depending on the quality and the binding. Actually, trail skis are somewhat cheaper at the lower end. You can buy laminated wood skis, bindings, and shoes in sets for about $100, but lower line versions of these already marginally adequate backcountry skis are not likely to get you in and out comfortably and safely.

Touring skis are heavy, probably heavier than they need to be for anything but the most rugged expeditionary work. This narrows our choice to good-quality fiberglass and wood laminated trail skis or Bushwhackers.

Both types have their advantages and disadvantages for backcountry outings. Trail skis move faster with less effort along smooth stretches of powder snow. They are quieter-running, so quiet you can hardly hear them whisper, which is an advantage to big game hunters and photographers. They are extremely light and can be hauled on the side of your pack without unbalancing your load.

Their principal disadvantages are their sensitivity to snow conditions and their fragility, even among the best. Also, their limitations in bindings are a severe handicap for backcountry trips which might involve several different kinds of terrain.

Bushwhackers, the bastard child of skis and snowshoes, will get you just about anywhere in just about any conditions. They are more maneuverable in tough blowdowns, bush, or rocky country, will stay aloft in a variety of snow conditions, and won't break without a very good reason. The metal edges allow the short, plump Bushwhackers to ply the slopes much the same as regular downhill skis, and they are light enough to pack.

The principal drawback of the Bushwhackers is the noise created by the plastic fish scales. It resembles a moving train wreck on hard, crusted snow. The racket can be reduced by a liberal rubbing with either straight candle parrafin or silicone stick; but no matter what you do, Bushwhackers shout when the wood-bottom trail skis whisper.

Bushwhackers also require more effort on the flats and trails than trail skis and they are not as fast in flat, open country.

I used the long, lean trail skis for many years, and found I had to replace broken or shriveled skis about every other year. I hunted with them gliding along the backcountry trails, and for the most part, I figured they had paid for themselves about the time I had to buy another pair.

About three years ago I tried a friend's pair of Bushwhackers and, although I had a little trouble standing for a few minutes because I couldn't stop laughing, I discovered immediately they opened a lot of new territory that was off limits to trail skis. I bought a pair and, two and one-half seasons later, they are scarred and battered but still healthy.

I had my Bushwhackers mounted with Silveretta Plate touring bindings, which currently cost about $45. The touring bindings allow me to use my mountaineering boots; so if snow conditions permit or snow conditions dictate (there are pitches that even Bushwhackers can't handle), I can carry the skis and go it on foot. The Silveretta Plates hinge at the toe, which means I can telemark—use the long, gliding step of cross-country skiing—or lock up at the heel for enough rigid support to downhill ski on the metal edges.

Bushwhacker skis currently cost about $100, which, when you

add on the cost of touring bindings and poles, pretty much chews up the $150 we allocated for skis earlier. The only additional equipment you will need for your Bushwhackers are a bar of common paraffin candle wax or silicone wax for soft snow conditions and two pieces of rope about three feet long to make safety laces between your legs and the bindings.

If you are already a downhill skier, converting your style to cross-country should not be much of a problem. If you don't ski but would like to find out what the backcountry looks like from a pair of skis, many sporting goods stores or ski shops will rent the necessary equipment.

Learning to ski from scratch is another matter; you can't hire it for the weekend. In many areas of the country private or class instruction is available and this is probably the best and fastest way to learn skiing. A skiing friend is also a resource that can be tapped or, if you are the bookish sort, there are several good books which, along with some backyard practice, will eventually get you on your skis and keep you there.

HORSE PACKING

Although this book is primarily concerned with backcountry pursuits on foot, there are a couple of modes of overland travel that are appropriate in some areas and concentrate the wear on the other parts of the anatomy.

A thin, meandering line of businesslike horses, alert riders, and stoic pack mules picking carefully through the rocks and cracks of a high mountain trail in a thick morning mist is perhaps the zenith of American outdoor sport. The horse packer travels in both time and space—miles from the smells and sights of civilization and centuries from the worries, frustrations, and technology of modern living.

These trails that lead from the space age back into time are becoming so rare they may soon be museum pieces. They exist only in a handful of wilderness or primitive areas and a few scattered national parks in the West.

It takes a lot of raw country to qualify—hundreds of thousands of acres of land that has not felt the saw or bulldozer, together with an assurance from society that it will be left in its primal

Horse Packing

Hunting on horseback is an expensive way to travel but it gives you an eagle's-eye view of the world that is difficult to get in any other way. (Drawing by Tony M. Sandoval)

condition forever. There are fewer than twenty such areas in the United States and when you take out the national parks, which can't be hunted, the sum drops to an even dozen. There are other primitive areas under federal management which are or may be candidates for wilderness classification, but getting Congress to make the final designation is a hard, uphill battle against powerful forces. Timelessness is a quality, not a quantity, and there are a lot of people who can't see value in any commodity that can't be added or subtracted.

Like anything that is rare and valuable, wilderness horse trails are expensive. A week on one with a professional packer and guide after big game can cost $1,000. Most outfitters offer less expensive excursions, but you can count on spending at least $500 for a one-week horse trip into the wilds.

Professional packers in wilderness areas are strictly regulated by both the U.S. Forest Service and state fish and game departments. They run a tight ship and give you your money's worth in services, which sometimes border on opulence.

The only things most packers don't provide on wilderness excursions are personal items such as clothing, sleeping bags, and the tools of your quest (rifle, camera, and fishing gear). Good outfitters pride themselves on seeing to every detail of a trip, and most of them would prefer their clients just settle into the business of enjoying the wilderness and leaving the work to the outfitter and his professional crew.

Virgil Burns, who operates a well-known lodge and camp out of Montana's Bob Marshall Wilderness Area, has some observations on how to spread the enjoyment of a wilderness horse pack trip around.

• Clients should take the time to pack all of the personal gear they will need to feel comfortable. This includes sleeping bag, enough appropriate clothing to last for the duration of the trip, stout footgear, toiletries, booze (which Burns insists be restricted to evenings around camp), and necessary sporting equipment such as rifle, ammunition, knife, binoculars, fishing tackle, and camera equipment.

• Clients should realize that game and fish are wild, not hand-fed domestic critters, and that bagging them requires a lot of work and some little luck. "Some people come out here with the impression there is a trophy behind every bush and if there isn't, the function of a guide or packer is to go out and herd one there. This simply isn't true. These are wild animals and wild fish and they have a strong interest in living. That is the way it should be and I hope most people wouldn't have it any other way."

• Stock and equipment are the better part of a packer's capital and his livelihood depends on their remaining in good, working condition. The animals are trained to work hard and packing equipment is built to absorb hard use, but neither will tolerate much abuse.

The care of animals and gear is the responsibility of the packer and his crew. "We certainly don't discourage an interest in the welfare of our stock but it is better if clients allow the hands to do most of the handling. They can recognize problems developing and know how to deal with them and besides, they are paid to do the work. I would prefer clients just concentrating on taking advantage of the country."

Burns, who operates the Bob Marshall Wilderness Ranch with his wife Barbara, enjoys one of the highest hunter success ratios in the state: 60 percent on elk and about the same on deer. "But I am lucky," Burns admits. "My hunters are all good at the sport, know game and work hard. They do it because they enjoy it and know it is the only way of filling their tags."

Burns runs his wilderness camp like a synthesis of a Caribbean luxury cruise and a sentence in the Siberian salt mines. The tents are warm and cozy, the food is luxurious, and the mood is light but serious. During the day the wranglers wrangle and the hunters hunt. "Nobody sits around camp. If they want to sit they can do that someplace else. If they came here to hunt, they hunt."

During the summer Burns outfits fishing and photographic tours of the Bob Marshall Wilderness which are both less expensive and more leisurely.

WATER TRAVEL

Floating, either by canoe or raft, as a backcountry mode of travel is restricted by the limited number of remaining navigable rivers that flow into remote areas.

Unfortunately, river drainages have always been especially attractive to road engineers for connecting this place with that place. Look at a map of just about any state and you will probably notice that many roads follow rivers and most rivers have a road alongside.

Wilderness Pack Train

Shown here is horse packer Virgil Burns bringing his hunting camp mules up Holland Pass to the Bob Marshall Wilderness Area. (Photo by Harley Hettick)

Worse, I am convinced that rivers are so compelling to road designers that they can't resist building roads along valleys even if they don't lead anywhere. Near Idaho's Selway Wilderness Area there used to be a lovely pristine stretch of the Lochsa River running for miles out of craggy hills to the Salmon River. One year a road suddenly appeared along most of this stretch. It led from barely anywhere to absolutely nowhere and appears to have no function other than promote the ruin of one of the most beautiful trout rivers imaginable.

If road builders don't ply their trades in backcountry riverbottoms, one of the numerous agencies that build dams will make puddles out of them. Most major rivers in the West and more than a few elsewhere have at least one dam, and some have been rendered into a series of pools with one reservoir ending at the face of the next dam upstream.

There are backcountry rivers that somehow have managed to escape asphalt and concrete. To name a few: the Rogue River in Oregon, the Upper Missouri River in Montana, the Yellow Dog River in Michigan's Upper Peninsula, the Salmon River in Upstate New York, several rivers in Maine, long stretches of rivers in West Virginia, Kentucky, and Tennessee, and byways in swamps in the Deep South. Some areas abound with wild rivers, but in most states it is going to take a major effort to find a suitable spot.

A backcountry river must first of all be navigable. It must be large enough to carry you and your craft with a tolerable number of portages and have accessible launching and landing areas. It must also flow through a large enough area to provide the backcountry experience you are seeking. It should either be of drinkable quality or have freshwater sources such as feeder streams which are pure. (This is not an absolute requirement; you can either purify drinking water or bring enough along, but it detracts from the backcountry experience if you can't drink the water you are paddling in.) The river or the surrounding land must have the fish or wildlife you are seeking.

I have left out lakes because as far as I know unsettled lakes are extremely rare. There are some in Maine and a few here and there along the northern tier of states, but most lakes are well known and well traveled and the presence of several other parties on an open lake tends to dim the magic of the backcountry adventure.

Canoes

Canoes are certainly among the most ingenious inventions of humankind. They perform well in fast, white water, lazy big rivers, or large wind-swept lakes. They are maneuverable, light for their carrying ability, can keep occupants and contents dry in all but the roughest water, and are infinitely water-worthy. They are the only way to go if you are considering a fall hunting trip or excursion because they have the capacity to haul big game and are not as inclined to ship water as are inflatable rubber rafts.

Canoes come in different sizes for different functions. They range in length from twelve to eighteen feet, in height above the

Canoe Travel

There is a lot of wild country along rivers, even in the lowlands, that can best be reached by water. And canoes are probably the best way of navigating rivers. (Drawing by Tony M. Sandoval)

waterline from eight inches to about a foot, and in width between two and one-half and three feet. Shorter canoes are normally intended for one person, whereas most seventeen-footers can handle three without much difficulty.

Low narrow canoes are streamlined for racing while higher, wider canoes are intended to manage heavy cargo and provide more protection from wind and current spray.

A backcountry river canoe for both hunting and fishing with two persons and gear should be at least sixteen feet long and have enough carrying capacity to accommodate both gear and game. It can be made of aluminum, fiberglass, cedar, or wood and canvas and should be designed for river use, which means a very small keel or no keel at all.

Prices of canoes generally depend on size and material. The cheapest are generally fiberglass, the most expensive cedar and canvas and wood. In the middle are aluminum and a new generation of plastics (such as ABS) which are proving tougher and lighter than fiberglass. The range starts at about $250 and doesn't end until it hits $1,000.

Most experienced hunters and fishermen avoid aluminum. An aluminum canoe is an elongated, upside down bell which amplifies the slightest twitch of the toe into a dull chime which fish can feel for hundreds of feet and animals can hear for a mile.

Purists prefer a wood and canvas canoe because of its handling qualities, but acknowledge this type is more delicate than others and admit it is atrociously expensive.

The new ABS plastics, such as Royalex and Kevlar, are gaining a lot of popularity among racers and full-time canoeing enthusiasts because they are light and nearly indestructible; but they cost more than you might think, around $500.

Fiberglass weighs a little more than the miracle plastics and is not quite as strong, but costs a great deal less. You can still buy a fifteen-foot glass canoe for about $175, but a good-quality seventeen-footer will run about $250.

Canoes, like skis, can be rented; but don't take a rented vessel down the river of no return without giving it a maiden voyage first. Canoes, like skis, require more background and practical experience than sitting through a few Deerstalker movies, and that rented canoe could be a cripple of the French and Indian wars.

The trick of canoeing on rivers is to let the vessel do most of the work while you keep a low profile. Keeping the center of balance low is the reason Deerstalker used to kneel on the bottom of his birchbark canoe during most of the late show. Modern canoes have seats or thwarts which are designed for sitting, but never, never allow your weight to get above them. In rough water it is a good idea to drop down into the kneeling position with your butt touching your heels to give the canoe a little extra stability.

The next thing to remember is to distribute weight, yourself and your gear, evenly along the keel or middle of the canoe and *never* let it shift to one side or the other.

On rivers, a canoe should ride with the bow (front) higher than the stern. This will allow the bow to track easier around water obstacles and present a higher profile in front against spray. Most canoes are laid out to facilitate this with the rear seat right on the stern transom, the middle seat (in a three-person canoe) slightly aft of midship, and the front seat a leg length from the bow transom. When you are packing gear into the canoe you can upset this balance by setting too much of the weight forward. Pack extra weight as evenly as possible from behind the front seat to the rear.

Rafts

Rubber rafting can be a real delight in the summer and a maritime disaster in the fall. Rafts, even the kayak-shaped variety, are not engineered to keep you and your gear dry on rivers. In the summer this is all right since it is too hot anyway but in the fall, when water and air temperatures are in the forties, it can be a one-way ticket to hypothermia.

The nicest thing about rafts (in the summer) is their portability. They are light and can be packed deflated long distances to pick up a river in the backcountry.

Rafts are also more forgiving than canoes. The squat, low-profile raft will roll with just about any punch and stay upright but it doesn't have the canny way a canoe has of avoiding rocks and snags. Consequently, rafts are subject to frequent deflation, and any extended trip should include an ample repair kit (with larger patching material and more glue than most makers provide with the raft). Unless somebody has awfully strong lungs, it is also wise to stash a foot pump on board to restore the raft to seaworthiness after patching.

Rafts are not as sensitive as canoes to the distribution of passenger or cargo weight. The primary consideration in stashing gear is to keep it as waterproof as possible. It is a good idea to wrap packs and dry gear tightly in plastic garbage bags and keep them off the floor of the boat by suspending them with ropes to the sides.

You might as well be reconciled to getting wet during a river trip in a raft; so wear easily dried clothes and remember to keep some warmies dry along with your camping gear.

Rafts come in a variety of sizes, shapes, materials, and prices. If you are going to pack your raft, weight becomes a prime consideration. There are some excellent lightweight two-man rafts available. One weighs just over ten pounds, is made of a tough impregnated fabric, and costs about $150. Two- or three-person kayak-shaped rafts made of heavy (but extremely vulnerable when warm) vinyl cost from $100 to $200 (depending on the material and size), weigh between fifteen and thirty pounds, and offer a bit more control than the standard doughnut-shaped craft.

The best paddles for rafts are the ferruled aluminum-shafted plastic affairs. They are inexpensive (about $10), light, and can be connected to allow one person to control the craft.

The tools and crafts of wilderness travel open virtually every type of backcountry terrain and condition to the foot-loose sportsman. All you need is the proper equipment with the knowledge to use it and any type of country, high or low, is your domain.

CHAPTER 4

All About Camping

The nature of camping has changed more than any other facet of backcountry travel during the past couple of decades. Hiking is still basically the same—stumble here, get swatted by a branch there—but the physical act of making a temporary home in the backcountry has evolved into a high art, a code of ethics, and a matter of technology.

ECOLOGICALLY SOUND CAMPING

In older camping literature, prior to about 1950, the hiker was shown how to saw, whittle, dig, and mason a lovely little glen into a luxurious home away from home. Elaborate stonework was required for a fireplace, branches were used for cooking implements and saplings for furniture. There was usually a large trough latrine complete with the corpse of a healthy young tree as a sitter. Beds were made like graves with a trench dug out of the ground covered with wreaths of fresh boughs. When the story book party left Mother Nature after two glorious days, they left her crippled and disfigured.

Today, this sacrilege is illegal in many areas and certainly unethical anywhere but at the city dump. A lot of people and creatures use the backcountry and it isn't fair for a few to maim it.

And with modern camping equipment there is no need to render the land a replica of the suburbs. You can now literally haul everything you need and a little of what you think you need on your back, set it up without disturbing more than a few blades of grass, and leave your campsite with all the magic you found in it.

Pros and Cons of Campfires

Most people today don't seem to have much trouble spending a few nights out without the marginal creature comforts of rustic sapling furniture or uptown toilets. But fires are a little bit harder for most of us to forego. Virtually every trail in the country is marked with circular stone or dugout monuments to campers past.

There is a lake high in the Missions which is one of my favorite jumpoff places for high adventure. It is a lovely pristine pool nestled in a glacial bowl, framed on three sides by high-arching mountain ridges. The circumference of this wilderness jewel is nearly a mile and every thirty feet or so, like an unneeded guidepost, there is a firepit. I have never seen more than two parties on the lake at the same time but, in the spirit of generosity, let's say as many as a dozen parties have camped there simultaneously. So why are there two hundred fifty fireplaces? Because everyone who goes there seems to feel compelled to erect a monument to himself.

When I camp there, which is seldom because I don't sleep well around all of these monumental achievements, I borrow somebody else's fireplace, then carefully dismantle it and replace the stones along the shore in the morning.

The friendly spark and glow of a campfire is compelling, and building fires is almost a reflex with most backcountry folks. However, fires do alter the nature of the land by scorching the earth, requiring a windbreak, and consuming green or dry fuels which have value other than fire fodder. There are backpackers who would just as soon burn their homes as light a campfire (for more or less the same reasons). But I, and most of the people I hike with, still stoke up an evening fire if we are convinced it will not leave a permanent wound on the land.

My own criteria for firemaking are an already existing fireplace or a rocky or sandy spot large enough to hold a fire without its spreading, or where a fireplace can be dismantled and the site restored to its pristine condition. I also keep my fires as small as their cooking and toe-warming functions will allow. This not only saves firewood and reduces the possibility of things getting out of hand; it also makes cleanup and restoration when I break camp much easier. A low, gentle fire is also easier to cook over and a fire that is engineered to just maintain glowing coals manages to stretch that magic moment throughout dinner and into the evening.

Camp Drainage

The rustic sages of yesteryear preached embanking or trenching the entire camp area to prevent runoff buildup in a storm. In the days when tents were normally bottomless pups or shelter halves this may have been marginally necessary, but with today's synthetically waterproofed, floored tents the practice of draining is superfluous and harmful. Nevertheless, draining has become a religious ceremony to some people, and you still see $150 watertight tents with elaborate storm sewer systems excavated around them.

CHOOSING A TENT SITE

Although modern waterproof bottomed tents don't require any ground preparation, there are a few lay-of-the-land rules that should be observed for a comfortable, dry night's sleep. You can expect drainage problems on a rainy night if you pitch in a dry arroyo or creek bed. Even a light rain will accumulate in these natural runoff channels. No sensible person would build a solid brick home in a flood plain, but it is surprising how many people will pitch a delicate tent in the path of flood waters. Find a spot that will remain high and dry during a rain.

The next consideration in a tent site is finding a floor-sized area that is relatively level. This doesn't mean you have to bring a transit or carpenter's level, but eyeball your spot at right angles to the growth of trees. If the spot slopes off in one direction, and it usually does, try to engineer the lie of the tent so it will pitch level from side to side and place your head higher than your feet. If the tent slopes from one side to the other, the person on the high side will spend most of the night rolling onto the person on the lower berth.

Now that you are dry and level, you can check your site over for the bumps, lumps, and thumps that don't seem like much in daylight but will take their toll later on. You don't have to be a princess to feel even a pine cone through a thin foam mattress; so be pretty careful about policing the barracks. The only way to be sure you got it all is to lie down and roll around on the floor.

Hip and shoulder holes can increase comfort by giving these awkward parts of the anatomy a place to rest at night, but they also require the disturbance of the ground. In sand or loosely consolidated forest duff a little sifting here and there isn't going to make an awful lot of difference, but if you have to break the harmony of a moss bank or grassland, the results will be visible for a long time.

If you are going to build a fire, make sure all this tent site preparation takes place far enough from the fire area to preclude the possibility of searing sparks eating holes in your shelter.

Look around your tent site for things that may fall on you during the night. Obviously, pitching under a talus slope or cliff might put you in the path of a rolling or falling boulder. In the winter, such a site might be buried in an avalanche.

Other, less spectacular nighttime phenomena can leave campers dreary-eyed and grumpy in the morning: snow or pine cones falling off overhead trees, a branch or twig that thumps or scrapes against the side of the tent all night, or furry creatures running to and from their den at the door of the tent.

There are nocturnal sounds, however, that are conducive to sleep: the rustling of breeze-blown leaves, the soothing nocturne of a stream, or waves murmuring along a lake shore. Streams and lakes will not only contribute a lullaby but will also provide a ready source of fresh water.

Availability of Water

Fresh water is so important to the comfort and safety of a back-country trip that it is wise not only to aim for a readily accessible supply of water as a destination (even if you are not fishing) but also route your trek as close to water as possible. Water always

Streamside Campsite
This light, unobtrusive, clean skiing camp is located by the banks of a creek.

takes the shortest and easiest course to get wherever it is going, and there is normally a game trail along a waterway. Wild furries appreciate an easy walk and an occasional sip as much as hikers; so why not follow along?

In the Rocky Mountains where I live and hike, and in most other mountain ranges, water that rises in the hills and flows down through roadless backcountry is always suitable for drinking and often so tasty that it is practically worth the trip just for a sip. But in other areas watersheds pick up enough contaminants from various commercial activities to make it wise to check on the quality of the water before setting out. State or federal foresters, fish and game wardens, or local outdoorsmen usually know whether water in the creek you will be following or in the lake where you will be camping is pure; but if there is a question, either change your plans or be prepared to boil or purify drinking water.

OUTDOOR TOILET ARRANGEMENTS

Now that you have water to drink, a place to cook your food and warm your body, and a shelter for the night, there is only one other human need you are going to have to consider in your backcountry camp: relieving bladder and bowels.

There is no need for fancy accommodations. As a matter of fact, I think most people can deal with the universal problem of bound-up backcountry bowels if they have the freedom to choose a spot that is comfortable to them. A convenient bush or tree is ecologically sound for urinating, and more elaborate measures to satisfy the modesty of a mixed group are probably inappropriate in the wilds.

Most people I know have trouble unplugging bowels in camp. My own trick is to drink a couple of cups of coffee, eat a bowl of oatmeal, and wait until the combination of the two hits bottom on the trail. Then I just take a break, find an appropriate spot (which is not overly well drained and will not disturb surrounding vegetation), dig a one-foot-deep hole with a trowel, and let nature take its course. Afterwards I cover the excrement and toilet paper. Both will deteriorate rapidly buried under a foot of soil and add nutrients to the ground. Next spring something may grow there that otherwise would not, and that is not something you can say about your septic tank or municipal sewage system back home.

EXPLORING AROUND CAMP

How much time you will have for afternoon or evening rambling around the neighborhood of your camp depends on how much time you allowed in your trip planning and how well you managed to hold your hiking pace. If you are fishing, you will want enough time after pitching a tidy, comfortable camp to hitch up the tackle and see about some fresh meat for supper.

Even if you aren't fishing, one of the backcountry's simpler pleasures is poking around the camp area, sans pack, to get a feeling for the neighborhood. Climb as high as you can get within reason above camp (you will be amazed at how much strength and dexterity you have without your pack), and take a look around. Take your map along to see if you can identify any of the local landmarks. An area that was marked as a swamp on the map may have been dammed up by beaver, creating a pond that nobody has ever bothered to investigate before; or you may find that a series of ledges on a nearby hill that looked unclimbable on the map would make it an easy walk up.

These free evening hours are also prime time for taking pictures. Most mammals in the wilds are nocturnal, and the chance of seeing them and getting pictures is much better when they are coming out of their lairs in the evening or going back in the early morning.

CAMP CHORES

The business of camp life—gathering wood and building a fire (if you intend to have a fire), cooking dinner, and washing up afterwards—should be divided among the members of the party. The division can be by function—somebody assigned to do a certain thing during every meal. Or it can be split by duty days, with one person having all the chores in one camp or during one day and having the next day or two off. I like the latter arrangement because I prefer to have a day or two completely on my own rather than have to hang around near camp until it is time to go to work.

CAMP MEALS

My own rule for camp meals (which usually means dinner and breakfast) is to do away with as much fuss and bother as possible without inciting a food riot among my companions. Therefore I rank the advent of freeze-dried trail foods as a technological accomplishment surpassing moon walking and electric tooth brushes.

Another reason I would prefer to be alternately saddled with all the camp chores, is that I don't want anybody to know just how little I have to do to prepare and clean up from one of my cele-brated epicurean delights. I merely boil water (no pot or pan to scrub), add it in the correct proportion to a plastic envelope or aluminum tray provided with the package, stash the steeping packages off to one side of the pit, and round up the eaters. Before they arrive I deposit the courses on their plates, rub a little charcoal around the outside of my hands for effect, and modestly accept the acclaim.

Afterwards I gather up the plates, and a few pots and pans to add to the effect, and courageously leave the warmth of friend-ship and fire to lightly rinse out the plates. If somebody notes, upon my return, that my absence was hardly long enough to account for cleaning up after such a meal, I reply that I get a lot of practice at home.

Freeze-dried vs. Dehydrated Foods

Freeze-dried vittles are like manna from heaven for back-country devotees. Not only are they light to pack and easy to pre-pare, but many of them are surprisingly tasty and most are suffi-ciently nutritious to sustain a party indefinitely.

They are a tad expensive compared to grocery store dehydrated foods. Mountain House meat entrees, for instance, cost an average of about $2 with vegetable side dishes running about $1. Servings are fairly generous, about sixteen ounces per reconstituted package, which means that a meat and vegetable entree will serve two persons amply at an average cost of $1.50 each.

Grocery store dehydrated foods are less expensive but also less nutritious and messier. Dehydrated soups, macaroni and cheese, and skillet dishes are standbys with many backpackers who are reluctant to invest in freeze-drieds and break comfortable old habits.

There is a lot to be said for the garden variety dehydrated foods. Depending on what you buy and what you are mixing with it, the package cost is only a fraction per serving of freeze-dried packages. Macaroni and cheese or skillet dinners, for instance, cost only about twenty cents per helping out of the package. However, most are a little insipid as they pour and are not really well-balanced meals; so most people add some tasty but expensive protein.

The new generation texturized meat-flavored vegetable protein adds both flavor and substance to packaged dehydrates but also adds cost. Imitation bacon, for instance, is about a dollar per four-ounce jar, which is only enough to flavor and bolster two entrees, each serving two people. Therefore the per serving cost of a dehydrated meal is increased by about twenty-five cents.

I have more or less forsaken dehydrated dinners in favor of freeze-drieds but have faithfully retained some of the grocery store lighter fare. Soups and bouillon require hardly any space at all to stash and taste good by themselves or as added flavor for other dishes. My favorite combination is Chinese noodles with a package of instant vegetable broth thrown in and a little instant egg mix added. For about thirty cents I can put a lot of tasty and wholesome filler into a couple of empty stomachs.

Tea, instant coffee, dehydrated milk, and cocoa are other market lightweights that can make meals worthwhile without busting the budget.

Hot vs. Cold Food

Although most people, including myself, regard a cozy and satisfying warm evening meal as indispensable in the backcountry, the opinion is growing among nutritionally minded hikers that trail food does not necessarily have to be warm and probably should be eaten proportionately throughout the day. The people who hold this view eat nothing but grains, granola, nuts, and dried fruit throughout the duration of a backcountry trip without apparent ill effect.

One of my frequent hiking chums took to a steady diet of squirrel food a couple of years ago. The only problem I have noticed in his trail behavior is my panting to keep up with him. He usually scouts around or gets in a half hour of fishing while I am either building a fire or stoking up the stove, then returns to camp to munch granola contentedly while I sup on the product of my lost half hour. I have found, however, that he usually weakens to the offer of some after dinner tea. Crawling into the sack with a warm stomach is, in the final analysis, the quintessence of backcountry life.

This fellow annoys me in many other small ways. One of the reasons he can travel faster than I is that his pack weighs only about half as much as mine. He doesn't carry a stove or fuel, never sleeps in a tent even in the winter (preferring to burrow into the snow instead), and manages quite well without all the precautionary gear, like extra clothing, that I find necessary. In spite of his spartan attitude about equipment, he never seems to loose a wink of sleep, even in a downpour, because he is clever about engineering waterproof shelters with his poncho. He never gets wet on a damp trail because he is small and can completely cocoon himself in the self-same poncho, and is never flagging in strength even on long, hard trips.

I have learned a lot during our weeks in the backcountry. I have learned that I can shave a few things off my back that I had previously felt were positively essential. I have learned how to eat more simply (although I still won't give up my hot evening meal). Most importantly, I have learned that discomfort is a relative thing and something one can become accustomed to. I still don't like sitting around for hours bound into a poncho envelope during a driving rain but I have found I can do it. I have discovered that I can still sleep even if rain has lapped over my poncho shelter and soaked the bottom of my sleeping bag, and I have found that the tennis shoes I always carry to relieve the traction my hiking boots put on my feet are not as necessary as I had thought.

Nix on Canned Goods

Getting back to food, the only kind of food I think is genuinely out of place in the backcountry is perhaps the most common there: canned goods. Twenty years ago cans were the only way to travel, but today they are excess baggage which all too often finds its way into the landscape. Many backcountry areas today are literally garbage heaps.

This love affair we have with metal containers is silly, especially in the backcountry. A 16-ounce can of chili weighs 17 ounces in the pack and takes up around 25 cubic inches of space. The same freeze-dried amount of chili in a 10-cubic-inch container weighs just 3.8 ounces (or about one-fifth of the weight of the canned product). Nutritionally they are identical. I actually prefer the taste, if not necessarily the texture, of the freeze-dried chili; the only advantage of the can is its price, about one-half of the $1.50 the freeze-dried costs.

Cans are a blight on the environment, coming and going. They require the mining of metals, which distrubs natural resources. Cans and petroleum-based plastic containers openly compete with wildlife and recreational use of the land and are an anathema to people who wish to enjoy these lands as wild backcountry.

Cans, for the most part, cannot be reprocessed, which means the discards you do haul down from the hills or throw away at home end up on or in the ground someplace.

Throwaway containers are another one of those technological miracles that have backfired because we haven't learned to use them properly. They most surely don't belong in the backcountry, on the ground or even in packs.

A GOOD NIGHT'S SLEEP

Most everybody who would bother to buy a book about wilderness sport has spent a night outdoors either as a backpacker, hunter, or fisherman, and is probably already aware of the sleeping bag insomnia syndrome. This common affliction occurs in an absolutely universal sequence and produces tiresomely predictable symptoms.

It starts when you crawl into the sack gloriously tired from your first day's exertions. Your body and mind are totally at ease from the wholesome fatigue of the day, a friendly and satisfying supper, and the somnolent mood of the backcountry at night. You doze peacefully into a kind of semitorpor for an hour or two, cozy and secure in the fluff of your sleeping bag. Then suddenly you become starkly alert, realizing that you have nothing to be content about and certainly nothing to feel secure about. You notice that you can't lie on one side very long without something beginning to ache, and every time you roll over is a trauma that brings you back to attention.

There are those noises outside the tent, a rustling in the bushes over by the door or a scraping on the fabric at the rear of the tent. You know that neither a grizzly bear nor wolf has been seen in these parts in a century; so why are they picking on you? Ha, you reassure yourself, that couldn't be a vicious wild animal; obviously it is just the breeze in the brush. Your conscious mind is at ease once again and you almost doze off when there is a sudden subconscious scream warning you that the same bear that mauled a camper in Yellowstone National Park two years ago is about to tear through the thin fabric of your tent to drag you off into the bush of rural New Jersey.

And so it seems to go all night long. Minor discomforts and terrors plague you until morning, when you crawl out baggy-eyed and weary, knowing that you must face a tough day in the backcountry with undercharged batteries. Veterans know they will sleep like a log the second night if they can survive a day of bleary-eyed stumbling after the first.

Sleeping bag insomnia is caused by several factors both real and imagined, which accumulate and synergize to torture weary backcountry travelers through a night of dazed terror. These factors include the inescapable fact that one-quarter of an inch of closed cell foam is not as soft as a Serta Perfect mattress at home, that uncustomary "overtiredness" that sleep always has a hard time overcoming, fear aroused by the black, foreboding backcountry, and the cramped confines of an unyielding mummy bag.

The first night usually acclimates backcountry sleepers to these conditions and the terror and torture melt away into a blissful slumber the second night. But what can you do to salvage the first night and the day after?

The easiest solution is not to worry about it. If SBS occurs, there is nothing much you can do about it but ride with the punches. I was a long-time sufferer but quit suffering when I realized that I was actually getting more sleep than I thought between the fits of wakefulness and that these fits can actually be quite pleasant if you make up your mind to enjoy them.

Star-gazing is a good way to while away the fits and render them both less traumatic and shorter. I always plan to learn my common constellations during SBS fits and study them carefully. I am usually down to about Pegasus and noticing that Jupiter is rising over the ridge to the east when everything goes blank. What seems to me like a minute later, insomnia grabs me again and I peer back into the sparkling globe to pick up where I left off, only to discover that Jupiter has arched halfway across the sky and that I have slept through the surfacing of Venus.

When I crawl out the next morning I am usually more upset about not remembering enough about what I had learned about the stars than about the restless night I had.

If this doesn't work and you wake up woozy and worried about keeping your balance between steps, you can always plan ahead to make the day after the first night less demanding. Plan to spend your second backcountry day loafing around the neighborhood of camp or fishing or shorten the distance to your second night's camp. The important thing is don't let sleeping bag insomnia throw you or ruin your trip.

STYLES OF CAMPING

There are two ways of thinking about a backcountry camp, both reflecting the nature of different backcountry quests and both being perfectly acceptable on ethical grounds.

The first is the idealized camp with neatly pitched tents, a conscientiously designed fireplace, a drying and fluffing line for clothes and sleeping bags strung out between two trees, easy access to water, and a well-thought out system of personal hygiene.

A tidy and well-organized camp of this nature usually takes some scouting around to find an appropriate lie which either already has a fireplace or can accommodate one without leaving the ground disturbed. It takes longer to pitch and is ideally suited for the routine of a protracted base camp while the party fishes or mulls around the neighborhood for a few days.

In a protracted camp food should be carefully stored in suspended bags and scraps should be burned or buried immediately in a dishwater hole. Human scents will accumulate over a few days and draw bears and other pests from far away. If everything is kept neat, clean, and tidy throughout your stay, firewood is gathered only from downed trees and snags, and the lives of the local flora are religiously respected, the spot will not be any the worse for your stay after you leave.

This is the kind of camp that backcountry memories are made of and leaving it is often like leaving home.

On the other extreme is the casual bivouac, a light camp you pitch where you find yourself when it is sleepy time. Simplicity is its charm, although it usually takes some practice to get used to not having everything in its place. It is ideally suited for big game hunting or photography because it does not create as much fanfare as a more elaborate camp and does not generate the odors or human aura of fires or food.

BIVOUACKING

Pitching a good bivouac is an art. The lie is usually less than ideal, although you don't need as much flat ground for a simple overnight stop as you would want for a protracted camp and you are usually working with more creative tools.

You can use tents in bivouacs, but a level spot large enough for the floor is required for a tent and you may not have the time to find such a spot when night is gathering and the stomach is growling. A tent fly, waterproof nylon shelter tarp, or poncho are the accepted tools of the quick camp artist; and being able to recognize a good bivouacking spot with ample materials for hanging a shelter is the mark of an accomplished master.

My chum, the dry food freak, has a faculty for using his poncho to cover a dry bed with the skimpiest of resources. His shelters always have a different geometric flare, following the lines of whatever trees, bushes, or rocks happen to be handy. And, as I

The Art of the Poncho-Shelter Bivouac

The difference between tenting and bivouacking is the amount of imagination required to find a suitable lay and pitch the shelter. (Drawing by Tony M. Sandoval)

noted before, he never gets wet or, if he does, it never seems to discomfort him.

The trick to pitching a shelter, I am learning, is to never allow yourself to develop preconceived notions of what a shelter should look like. If it comes out an umbrella with a stake in the middle, what could be more appropriate. A dome following the arch of a downed snag could hardly be more modern. Of course there is always the V-shaped cross-section made famous by ancient woodsy lore, or the classic awninged shelter half of the same credentials. The only requirements are enough room under it to crawl around and provide shelter from the rain and taut anchors on at least the four corners. It should also be large enough to cover the full length and breadth of its occupants, and the canopy tight enough to repel rain or dew without forming puddle pockets.

The Game-stalking Bivouac

With the shelter pitched and sleeping bag unrolled, the next order or priority is seeing to dinner. As nice as fires are, as well as they cook meals, as heartily as they raise the spirits and as toasty as they warm the fingers and toes, they are totally out of place when you are trying to find big game. A fire in the backcountry is like starting a rumor at a church picnic; within minutes every furry within miles knows where you are, who you are, and what you are doing and will go to a great deal of trouble to see to it your paths don't cross.

There are two alternatives to fire: dry cold foods, a notion most people will have a little difficulty stomaching, or a stove. Of the two, dry foods are without a question the less disturbing to surrounding wildlife because they have very little odor themselves and require no additional aroma in their preparation.

Stoves, no matter how clean-burning and efficient, generate their own acrid smell. Light one in an enclosed area and find out how offensive they are to your relatively insensitive olfactories. But some stoves are stinkier than others. Kerosene burners are probably the most offensive, producing a heavy vapor which tends to hold its ground more stubbornly than exhausts from other fuels. Gasoline, white and stove gas, stinks when it is first lit and burning poorly, but its vapors are lighter and rise quickly. An efficiently burning gas stove produces hardly enough odor for humans to detect, although I am sure nose-sensitive animals have no trouble detecting it at short distances.

The least odorous stoves are the butane or similar compressed gas cartridge burners. They start clean and burn at least as clean as liquid gas stoves and are not as inclined to run roughly as do other stoves.

There is no way of masking all human odors; you are generating them all the time. Animals that depend on their nose to survive could smell you a long way off just after you jumped out of your morning shower. Masking scents, buck lure masks, and the like may confuse animals at a distance; but they seem to know there is something threatening behind all the perfume and keep a respectable distance.

The point is: you are already giving your quarry fair advance warning with your body; so why amplify your disadvantage by adding camp sights, sounds, and especially smells? A stalking bivouac should be as neat and clean as you can make it. If you do stove-cook your food, make sure plates are cleaned immediately after eating and that scraps and dishwater are buried deep enough to prevent odor from escaping. Fold food packaging, foil, plastic, and paper into a plastic garbage bag and wrap it tightly. You will be carrying this out with you; so find a snug corner in your pack where it will stash nicely and can be found easily after dark.

Stoves should also be carried in plastic bags. The air-tight plastic will prevent escaping fuel from wicking into other equipment and it will keep the gas smell tightly locked in your pack. Wait until the stove has cooled; then wrap it up and either put it in your pack or someplace you can find it easily in the morning for breakfast.

Other necessary people odors such as body wastes, even urine (which any dog worth his salt can smell 100 feet away after 3 days), should be conscientiously buried. Unnecessary human fragrances such as deodorant, cologne, alcohol (a bad number in the backcountry anyway), and tobacco should be forsaken for more appropriate times.

Most all woodland mammals and virtually all big game species have excellent hearing, thank you, and constant noise is another distinctly human commodity in the backcountry. Rattles, clatter, and voices are nearly as dead a giveaway as scents and should be kept to an absolute minimum. Items which rattle, such as metal pots and spoons, should be well packed and insulated in your pack; in camp they should be stored where people aren't going to be stumbling over them in the middle of the night. When cooking, be conscious of the clank and clatter your utensils make against one another and the stove and try to keep it down.

You can, of course, talk during a bivouac but not louder than is necessary to be heard. An uproarious laugh may compliment a keen wit but it will make the wildlife scoot.

Breaking or chopping sticks for pitching a shelter is a cal-culated risk. The sudden loud crack of a stick in the backcountry is not necessarily a human-identified sound, but it puts game animals on the lookout for other signs of danger. A really clever shelter craftsman can usually either find a stick of the right length or discover other less noisy ways of getting a strong pitch.

Game animals also use their eyes as defense by looking for motion and flash. Move around the bivouac slowly. Don't leave garments in places where the wind can turn them into danger flags and, by all means, if you do cook with a stove, find a sheltered spot where the flame is not going to be reflected against every tree and leaf in the area. A fire or its reflections is a warning signal to all wildlife.

The important thing to remember about a game-stalking bivouac is that it is just that—a rest stop during a stalk. You would not bang a gong while stalking nor would you blow smoke downwind or jump up and down. A bivouac is just an extension of the stalk; so don't break the mood just because you are stop-ping for an extended rest.

I haven't really kept track but I think I have seen more furries, game and non-game, at daybreak after a quiet bivouac than at any other time of the day. More than once I have started out of my shelter at dawn's first light to find deer and once even a cow elk staring back.

SHAKING DOWN

One way you can be assured of a smooth camp or bivouac is to know what to expect of your gear ahead of time. Pitching an un-familiar tent in the gathering gloom or trying to start a new stove after dark can turn a quiet camp into a hoedown complete with do-si-dos and hoots and hollers.

If you are a backpacker and are familiar with all your gear, pitching it at night would probably not be much of an exotic ex-perience. But if any of your gear is new, it pays to go out in the backyard and assemble it several times until you can do it blind-folded. Better yet, take an overnight shakedown hike nearby to pit all your skills and equipment against the demands of the land. Try orienteering with your compass and map, work out a hiking pace, and put all your camping gear through its paces. This may seem like small potatoes but it can save a lot of time, energy, and self-recrimination later.

CHAPTER 5

Wild Fish

There is no difference between fishing in the backcountry and fishing in the lap of civilization except backcountry fish are dumber and the tackle you will use need not and should not be as elaborate.

Wild fish are not actually congenital dopes. They trace their lineage back to the same sources as their slicker cousins in the lowlands. Rather, like the creatures of Eden, they are innocent to the ways of evil.

Fish are not born smart. The most wily brown trout who inhabits the celebrated and overfished stump hole in everybody's favorite trout river is not actually smart. No matter how many flies he resists or how old he gets resisting them, he will never be able to read Shakespeare, appreciate Beethoven, or even solve the simple abstract problems that a mouse can. He has, however, developed a reflex for discrimination. Conditioned by past pains, anxieties, and traumas, he recognizes man and his wares as dangerous and has refined an ability to distinguish minute differences in his food.

Fishing Trip Baggage

Shown are the essentials of a backcountry fishing expedition. The pack, in this case a Kletterworks self-forming soft pack, will contain: fly rod, reel, flies, summer weight sleeping bag, tennis shoes, rope, watch cap, wool palm socks, two extra pairs of wool socks, poncho, down vest, walking cap, sweater, sweatshirt, extra pants, knife, stove, fuel, fire bag, emergency kit, cooking set, toilet paper, extra matches, maps, compass, foam pad, and tent.

That difficult old brown will not only ignore your painstakingly tied imitation of a *Baetis* dun while feeding on the naturals, he will also reject another natural mayfly dun which differs only slightly from the *Baetis*. He has learned from past experiences that variety in his meals is not always conducive to good health. Once he knows a specific insect or food is both satisfying and safe, he will stick to it with remarkable intolerance to even slight variation. The more experience a fish has with the wiles of humankind, the more discriminating he becomes and the less credulous are his reactions to well-dressed fakes.

Wilderness fish, those who inhabit waters far from the pall of civilization, don't have the experience with fishermen or their spurious food to develop this discrimination. Even large wilderness fish are inclined to eat anything that faintly resembles food no matter how unreasonable it looks or behaves.

This does not mean wild fish cannot be conditioned to discriminate. It is quite remarkable, almost enough to make you believe in Walt Disney again, how quickly these backwater yokels can pick up a healthy dose of caution. That beaver pond my Upper Peninsula friend and I discovered in chapter 3 is no longer, he reports, the cradle of innocence it once was. Those brookies are now scholars worthy his most erudite artifices.

There is another reason why backcountry fish tend to eat first and ask questions later, especially in the mountains. Mountain climates are, within limits, hostile to finny and furry inhabitants, so the wildlife must adapt to unfavorable conditions. In the western mountains, for instance, an extremely energy-efficient trout known as the cutthroat evolved to survive the long cold winters in a semidormant condition on the fats stashed away during the brief harvest season.

Consequently, during the brief season of plenty, which at 10,000 feet lasts from about the end of June to the first of September, these remarkable fish must accumulate most of their annual supply of groceries. Cutthroats have a reputation of being dumb. They are, but not any more so than other fish. They are just hungry—hungry from the past ten months of starvation and hungry in anticipation of another five-sixths of a year without food. Alpine lake cutthroats can't afford to be too choosy about what they eat during their brief feast, and just about anything thrown at them will be accepted gladly.

This situation also exists to a lesser degree in the food-deficient native waters of brook trout. Brookies in Upper Michigan, New York, and Maine, also celebrated for their silliness, must survive hard winters on the little their habitat offers during the temperate seasons.

These two factors combine to make most backcountry fish both hungrier and less sophisticated than fish of the same species who live on the fringe of civilization. Although the feast and famine cycle may not be as pronounced in the backcountry homes of other game fish such as largemouth bass and pike, it probably does play at least a limited part in their environment.

In the lowlands, it is virtually impossible to fish out or destroy the population of a lake or stream by angling. A nucleus breeding population, or what biologists call a security threshold, capable of restocking fertile valley waters to their environmental capacity, will always remain, no matter how many fisherpeople try to wipe them out.

Pesticides or other chemicals, drastic changes in the water chemistry, or devastating land use alterations can wipe out good fishing waters. However, there is strong evidence that a healthy population in a healthy environment cannot be fished out.

This is not necessarily true in the backcountry, especially in the thin, pristine waters of the uplands. The very purity of an alpine lake or the upper fringes of a brook trout stream tributary is a factor that limits the density of fish populations and can affect the ability of surviving stock to recover from severe decimation.

A high alpine lake, for instance, which provides a limited quantity of fish food for a few months each year, has the capacity to support only a critically thin population. Sometimes this maximum capacity, which is the total life-sustaining capability of the water, and the minimum security threshold represent about the same number of fish. Thus the removal of a creelful or so can tip the balance of the water into inexorable moribundity; there are simply not enough fish remaining to survive the natural rigors and successfully spawn.

When you find such a gem, treat it as a rare and delicate piece

of art. Admire it, even use it, but don't deface it. You are probably too far from home to bring fish back without their spoiling;
so keep only what you can eat at the next meal and supplement
them with the food you brought in. Carefully return any others
you may catch, remembering they may be pregnant with the life-
future of the water. Remember also that it is no honor to kill more
of anything than you can eat—especially silly, hungry fish who
are eating their Thanksgiving supper.

FINDING WILD FISH

Not all backcountry water contains game fish. Some ponds,
lakes, and feeder fingers have already been decimated by man or
nature. Some may contain undesirable rough species, or extremely remote conditions may have precluded the introduction
of fish populations.

I know some perfectly lovely beaver ponds in Upstate New
York, far from the maddening crowd, which contain only stunted
dace, not a very sporting fish and certainly not an epicurean's
delight. I have hiked miles up naked stone ledges to locate small,
out-of-the-way alpine lakes in Montana's Rocky Mountains only
to find them shallow (which means they freeze solid every winter)
and naturally barren. I have trudged my way up to perfectly
splendid alpine fisheries only to find somebody had beat me to
them and "I should have been here yesterday."

In the Mission Mountains there is a lake formed by the junction of two towering mountain ridges. It is accessible only by a
stiff and dangerous 2,000-foot climb from one direction or a long,
high haul from another. Although I had known about the lake for
some time, an old Indian friend of mine informed me that in 1935
he and a bunch of friends had shinnied up there and spent three
days catching huge stupid cutthroats. On the way down one of
them was killed in a fall, but that only served to whet my
appetite.

I assumed that if the fishing was good in 1935 and the route
both tough and dangerous, it still should be good. On a bright
August weekend I stalked off loaded with ropes and mountaineering this-and-thats (all of which I found necessary) and after

much sweat and toil reached the near shore of what I can honestly describe as the most beautiful body of water I have ever seen. It was wedged tight between the cliffs of the two massive ridges like a precious jewel in a rare setting. The opposite end disappeared into a long, steep bank that was the foundation of a massive snow-topped mountain which stood sentinel over it all.

As soon as I caught my breath, I dumped my gear, unpacked my fly tackle, and began working my way along the shore. An hour and three or four hundred yards later I hadn't seen or felt a thing but figured the lusty inhabitants were taking an afternoon siesta to gather strength for a monumental evening rise. As the casts accumulated and the sun passed over the west ridge, I began to doubt. Finally I reached the opposite end and there, like an ancient burial mound, lay a heap of garbage consisting mostly of aluminum pudding tins and beer cans. Around this bleak marker were the signs of a fairly recent protracted camp—heavily compacted earth, tent ditches, the remains of a black plastic shelter, the stumps of the area's rare trees, and no less than three stone fire rings.

To this day I don't know how they got all that junk up there when it was all I could do to pull my flesh and the few necessary items of survival to the top. There are rumors that forest fire lookout helicopters are being used to take "sports" into virgin mountain lakes and supply them for a month, and I strongly suspect this is the solution to the mystery.

To make a sad story outrageous, I spent the better part of three days there watching and clambering around the landscape, fishing often and carefully with not so much as a good snag. The weather was fine, the barometer high, and the moon was in its last quarter. If there had been fish in there, they would have shown. The people ahead of me had seen to it that the paradise they found was a biological desert by the time they left. May the stocks in their portfolios fail, the fish in their creels rot, and their helicopters run out of gas.

For whatever reasons, backcountry waters that ought to have fish sometimes don't, and there is no way of really knowing. You can be relatively sure the upper backcountry stretches of a stream that contains fish below will offer some sport. This usually includes feeder lakes and tributaries unless there is some insurmountable obstacle such as a high dam or waterfall between the known quantity and the unknown.

In lowland backcountry, lakes are often isolated from sources of running water. These "pothole" lakes are fed and drained by ground water and fish or other aquatic forms of life have no way of getting to them. Often as not these lakes were barren in aboriginal times (although they could be remnants of larger bodies of water which left a balance fishery when they receded) but have had fish introduced by one means or another. The only way of telling for sure is to pack in and try them.

There are ways of tilting the odds in your favor. Most state conservation or fish and game departments have fairly comprehensive inventories of fisheries under their jurisdiction. If the lake shows on a map, they should be able to tell you what to expect. State or local offices of conservation departments should also know what condition an upcountry stream-connected lake is in or which backcountry river tributaries are likely to produce. Local sporting goods stores have a wealth of information and local sports clubs can sometimes add helpful advice (although local sportsmen are usually at least somewhat proprietory about their favorite water and might give you a bum steer).

A topo map of the area you intend to prospect will usually tell you whether a lake is stream-fed or a sink hole, or if a stream has any barriers between a downstream fishery and its wandering through the backcountry. A solid blue line on a topo means a perennial stream. A dotted blue line means a stream that dries up either seasonally or on occasion.

You can spot a waterfall on a topo the same way you spot cliffs. When the elevation lines are congested in an area over which the stream flows, you know it drops quickly. If the lines actually come together, there is probably a waterfall; narrowly spaced lines mean a sharp cascade is likely. If two lines on a seven and one-half-minute map come together, it means the straight drop of the fall can be anywhere from twenty to sixty feet. Many trouts and salmon can surmount a twenty-foot drop but if there are more than two lines blending, you are dealing with heights no fish can master.

Dams or irrigation weirs are usually well marked on maps, and the height is indicated in black print. The same migration rule that applies to waterfalls holds for dams, although often fish are either provided ladders to climb over the dam or reservoirs above the dams are planted. Check with conservation officials to find out.

TROUT

In general, but not always, wild backcountry fish are natives, that is, their ancestors were here before yours. They are the descendants of aboriginal stock and live where they do because they have evolved a way of dealing with the habitat.

Cutthroat trout (*Salmo clarkii*), as we have already noted, are the fish of high alpine lakes. They are one of two true trouts that inhabited the United States naturally. Rainbows are the other. Brook trout are native but not actually trout, as we shall see later. Cutthroat are closely related to the rainbow, and are widely distributed in subspecies throughout the West.

The West Slope cutthroat inhabits most of the northwest uplands from Colorado north and west to the Pacific Ocean. The distinctively spotted Yellowstone cutthroat is found on the east slope of Yellowstone National Park and the high tributaries of the Yellowstone River. The California golden trout was originally found in only one stream of the Sierra Nevada but has since been distributed more widely.

All the cutthroats can be easily recognized by the tell-tale red slashes just under their gills.

The celebrated rainbow trout (*Salmo guardinarri*) was originally found only as a resident of rivers and inland lakes of the Pacific West. Its range now includes just about every state in the United States and several areas of Britain and Europe. It is extremely tolerant (for trout) of heat and chemical conditions in water and requires a good deal of nourishment to thrive. Therefore it is usually found in lower water in the West and the rich waters of the Midwest and East.

Although rainbows are not native to backcountry rivers and lakes in the East, they have been established there long enough to become truly wild fish. In good condition they can be the best sporting fish among the trouts and grace any camp dinner.

Despite the fact that the range of the brook trout (*Salvelinus*

Dinner Fish
These rainbows were taken from the inlet of an alpine lake in Montana.

fontinalis) has grown well beyond its original territory—the northeastern seaboard, the Upper Peninsula of Michigan, and eastern Canada—its preferred habitat has dwindled. Like the cutthroat, the brookie is truly a fish of the backcountry. It evolved from the charr family in the naturally acid, pure waters of the northern woodlands and prefers water with the bittersweet taste of tannic acid. It cannot tolerate even the mild nutrient pollution that rainbows and brown trout thrive in.

Although it has been introduced to most of the northern tier of states, the brook trout lives only in the backwaters of those areas which meet its rather demanding needs.

Brookies—like their kin the lake trout, Dolly Varden, and kissing cousin brown trout—spawn in the fall and are normally somewhat gravid all during the summer. It is a good investment to temper your summer appetites in these fish, especially the brookie, because every female that survives the summer is worth at least one thousand fry in the fall. As an investment, that is a pretty good return.

All of these fall spawners begin to show vivid and distinctive sexing characteristics as fall draws near. The males, especially brookies, assume a color more garish than the females and develop protruding hooks on their lower jaws. Identifying and killing only enough males for dinner is one way to "have your cake and eat it too." One male can fertilize the eggs of several females on the spawning beds; so the loss of a few bucks during the summer isn't going to affect reproduction in the water.

The Dolly Varden or bull trout (*Salvelinus malma*) is a relative of the brook trout inhabiting only a few drainages on the west side of the Rocky Mountains and the Upper Missouri on the east side. Although they aren't the most handsome fish—usually long and leathery with wide, pikelike jaws—they grow very big indeed for a river fish (up to twenty pounds) and live in some of the nicest backcountry waters around.

The third charr in the continental United States, the lake trout (*Salvelinus namaycush*), is found only in large, deep lakes and is therefore hardly a backcountry angling candidate.

Although the brown trout (*Salmo trutta*) is a European import, it has taken over much of the trout water in the United States and has, in fact, salvaged some water that would no longer be inhabitable by other trouts. The stoic brown has a higher tolerance for organic contaminants than any native and can tolerate warm water, up to seventy degrees, for longer than the other trouts. In fact, browns do not normally thrive in the pure, thin waters of brookies and cutthroats, preferring waters that produce more food for a longer span of months.

The brown, then, is not the most likely backcountry fish. It is, however, found in the backwaters of many eastern and midwestern drainages; and in some areas of the lower Midwest, such as Missouri's Ozark Mountains, going back for browns is about the only respectable trout fishing available.

SALMON

The landlocked salmon (*Salmo salar*) and his seafaring cousin, the Atlantic salmon, now have a range extending from Maine north along the Canadian Maritime Provinces. The landlocked salmon populates a few central Maine lakes, where he is accessible only to backcountry hikes or canoeing trips. The anadromous (sea-running) Atlantic salmon has recently been reintroduced to the Narraguagus River in Maine, which does, to a limited extent, offer some backcountry fishing for this most famous sport fish.

On the West Coast, from northern California all the way to Alaska, there are several species of salmon which live about the same existence as the Atlantic salmon. These fish, from the tiny kokanee to the giant 100-pound Chinook, run the coastal rivers from the sea only once to die as kelts in their own nursery tributaries. Many rivers along their spawning migration route in California, Oregon, and Washington wind their way through truly splendid backcountry accessible only by river craft or foot.

SMALLMOUTH BASS

Most of the East and Midwest was the native home of the smallmouth bass (*Micropterus dolomieui*), and it can still be found in many backcountry areas throughout this region.

The smallmouth is a remarkable fish, thriving in a variety of waters from cool, fairly quick rivers to tepid freshwater ponds.

Brace of Brown Trout
These two fish accepted an invitation to a camp meal beside a river in upstate New York.

Groundwater-fed potholes are a good place to find it. Smallmouth bass can also be found in rambling mountain brooks throughout the lower Midwest and southern Appalachian states. Anybody who has fished for a variety of sport fish will attest the smallmouth is one of the gamest fish in North America; some feel it is one of the tastiest.

LARGEMOUTH BASS

The largemouth bass (*Micropterus salmoides*) is a native monster of the Deep South which has spread throughout the United States. It is entirely different from the smallmouth and can be easily distinguished by its relatively larger mouth, which extends back beyond its eyes, and eight, rather than nine rays in its dorsal fin.

In its range and element, the largemouth becomes large indeed, up to fifteen pounds. Trophy-size largemouth bass can still be found in the marshes and bog ponds of the South which are open to flatboating and canoeing.

NORTHERN PIKE AND SAUGER

The last but not the least of our backcountry fish is the northern pike (*Esox lucius*) and its southern relative, the sauger. The pike can pack a lot of weight into its lean, mean frame, up to forty pounds of carnivorous ferocity. It now inhabits nearly every major drainage in the northern United States.

Pike also inhabit large lakes and even some surprisingly small ponds. I remember a small five-acre pond a college friend and I found while hiking along the shore of Lake Michigan in central Michigan. It was May and the pond was virtually teeming with something, although the fish wouldn't come in close enough for a good look. We dumped our gear and began fishing with small spinning plugs on ultralight tackle. Every cast produced a strike but when we set back all we got was an empty line flagging in the breeze. These symptoms indicated pike but we didn't have any steel leaders. It took us four brimming boxes of lures to land about a half-dozen of the razor-mouthed spawners, including one five-pound keeper.

We returned to the pond other times that summer but got only a few strikes and an occasional small pike. It wasn't until the following May that we struck gold again (this time equipped with steel leaders) and an honest seven-pounder.

The pond was apparently a nursery of some kind inhabited most of the year with fry and adolescents. In May it was a favorite singles spot for ripe pike to do their thing.

There are many other worthy fish that inhabit backcountry waters. They include bream in the South, bluegills and crappies in the Midwest, whitefish and Grayling in the mountain West, and yellow perch just about anywhere. Although these are not the fish dreams are made of, they are hardy, practical fish that fight hard and taste good.

TACKLE

Objectively speaking, the requirements for backpacking tackle should be about the same as the rest of your backcountry packing gear—light, efficient, and eminently compact. Although the people who make tents, sleeping bags, and stoves have succeeded in designing and marketing products that meet all of these requirements, the firms who make fishing tackle haven't. In fact, they haven't even come close.

Fly Fishing Tackle

There are two generic forms of tackle for backpack fishing: fly tackle for appropriate places and species and spinning tackle for everything and everyplace else. The deficiencies in modern backpacking tackle are especially manifested in fly tackle, where a long, well-balanced, and well-distributed rod is essential. The problem, apparently, is breaking the rod in several sections to make a smaller carrying package. With the addition of a ferrule for each multiple section, the weight of the rod increases disproportionately, and there is a corresponding decrease in the essential liveliness of the action.

Manufacturers of fly rods who even bother with backpacking models compensate for this in two ways: (1) by totally ignoring these deficiencies and marketing breakdown pool cues masquerading as fly rods, or (2) starting with a shorter rod, seven-foot or under, and breaking it into four sections to come up with an overall packing length that is marginally tolerable to backpackers.

Although neither of these engineering solutions is really acceptable, the former, which is the more common, is totally out of the question. A useless rod is of no use no matter how tidy a package it comes in. The seven-footer that breaks into four sections (about twenty-three inches total packing size) is at least a known quantity that can probably perform a limited function well.

Most backpack fly fishing requires a longer rod to handle brushy lakes where a lot of line control is necessary. The rod should be long enough to steeple a high backcast over shore obstructions. This means a minimum eight-foot five- or six-line rod. The only good commercially manufactured eight-foot pack rods that I know of, and believe me I have looked, are a sweet brace of four-piece fiberglass rods called "Trailblazers," made and distributed by Streamside Anglers of Missoula, Montana. One is an eight and one-half-foot for six-line, the other eight-foot for five-line. Both of them are light, fine, and cast nicely but break into rather awkward twenty-eight- and twenty-six-inch packages respectively. The metal carrying tubes furnished with the rods will not fit into most backpacks and have to be strapped to the outside, where they are subject to weather and banging around. All things considered, these rods are a good buy at $59.95.

A lot of backcountry fishermen have gone through the pack rod routine and decided it is easier to put up with hauling their conventional two- or three-piece rods. However, if you try to strap a four-foot mast on your pack you are going to find that it catches in every low bush, grabs branches, and bangs on rocks. A better way is to put it in a stout carrying tube and redesign the tube as a walking stick. Stuff cotton or foam rubber in the bottom and glue a piece to the lid to absorb the shocks of the trail. Wrap the top with adhesive or rubber for a handle and tape a stout piece of cord at the top and bottom for a sling. When you don't need your hands it is a convenient third foot and when you do, just sling it across your shoulder.

I carried a two-piece glass rod walking stick fashion for a long time and was all right until I got into steep rock cliffs where elbow room became a matter of good health. I had wanted a shorter rod to fish small alpine meadow brooks; so I made a glass rod that was short, light, reasonably responsive, and would convert from an eight-footer to a six and one-half-footer. It doesn't cook fish or monitor my biorhythms, nor is it quite as sweet as the Leonard eight-foot bamboo I use down below, but it does both of its jobs efficiently, better than any other packrod currently available, thank you.

I started out with four run-of-the-mill fiberglass blanks—two

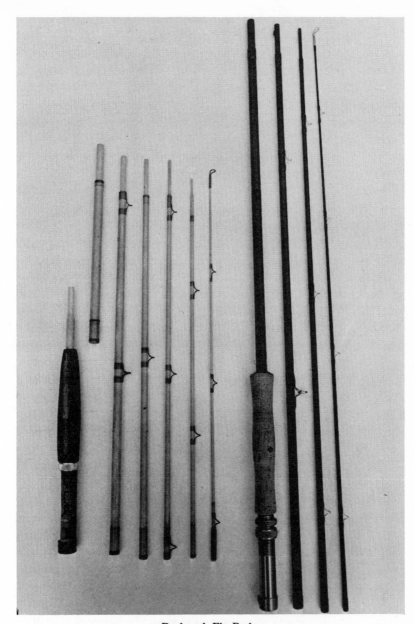

Backpack Fly Rods

At left is a homemade affair broken down into its six sections. It will fish either as an eight-footer or a six and one-half-footer depending on how the handle is set up with the lower sections. At right is an eight-foot four-piece fiberglass rod by Streamside Anglers.

thin-wall eight-foot flyrod blanks and two thick-wall six-foot spinning blanks. The whole bundle cost about $16.

I wanted the breakdown package not to exceed twenty inches in the case; so I worked out a number of formulas and came up with a six-section rod, each section measuring sixteen inches. To this I added the extra necessary one and three-quarters inches for the male sections of the glass ferrules and another quarter of an inch in packing. This breaks down into a total package length of eighteen inches. By eliminating one of the sections, I calculated, I could have a six-foot-four rod for brushy streams and such.

Assuming that Murphy's law is universally valid and would apply to fishing tackle as well as wars, I took my micrometer downtown and measured the diameter of several glass-to-glass rods at the ferrules while patient sporting goods clerks measured me for a straitjacket. The time and damage to my already unsavory reputation was worth it because I found there is more to glass rod building than just stacking the sections on top of one another. There is at least a five-one-thousandths-inch drop between the male-sectioned blank and the female-sectioned blank. The drop is designed to compensate for the taper of the male ferrule.

With a hacksaw I chopped the top blank at an even sixteen inches, then added a quarter of an inch to all the succeeding sections. At the bottom, I went back and cut the added one-quarter-inch off the top or male ferrule end of each of the sections, which gave me the five-one-thousandths-inch drop I needed.

The next step was tricky—matching the faster taper of the spinning rod blank, which I would be using for ferrules, to the slower-tapering fly rod. I started from the fifth or next to the top section, poked the spinning blank into the top of the male joint as far as it would go, and drew a line around the spin blank at this point. Then I took it out and poked into the fly rod tip section (which would be the female joint). The fit was about one-eighth-inch higher on the spin rod blank than the line I had drawn; so I knew I was in business. I cut the ferrule blank one and three-quarters inches above the line and two inches below it.

Next step was to smear epoxy glue around the top two inches of the fifth section and slide the ferrule, small end first, into the bottom of the section, pushing it home with the cut-off section of the spin rod blank. The ferrule seated well and, after the cement had dried, made a perfect fit with the tip section.

I repeated this process all the way down to the handle and had myself an eight-foot, six-section rod. But what about the six and one-half-footer? Read on.

The only section I could remove without distorting the action of the smaller rod was the bottom section, but of course I couldn't just throw that away because I had nothing else to hold onto. So I cut the handle off the bottom section, ferruling it to fit back in and adding a second ferrule within the first to fit the bottom of the third section. Now to convert it to the six and one-half-foot creek rod, I simply removed the top of the bottom section and the second section and slipped the handle into the third section.

By the time I finished I was ready for a section eight but I had my basic five-line eight-footer (actually measuring eight feet three inches) and convertible five-line six and one-half (which, when the dust settled and the glue had set, measured six feet four inches). I glued on an all-cork handle with sliding bands to save weight, wrapped the ferrule ends and guides with clear nylon thread, and epoxied over the thread winds. The rod is so ugly no self-respecting porcupine would touch it, but it has been thrilling and delighting backcountry fish for two years and beauty is as beauty does.

There are several good fly reels available for backpackers. Cortland makes an incredibly light graphite reel for about $35, or you can spend twice that much on an elegant Hardy Lightweight. If your money is more important than the figure you cut in the backcountry, try a $10 Japanese copy of a Hardy. They are available just about anywhere and work hard for long hours.

Although I prefer double-tapered flylines in lowland fishing, I use a forward-taper line in my backpacking outfit. The advantage offered by the forward taper is its ability to generate quick energy with a shorter casting line; that, in the obstacle-cluttered backcountry, can be a real advantage.

Backcountry flies are easy and won't require any major cash outlay. Those gaudy old trout flies you got hooked on when you first took up the sport but have since hidden in your closet from embarrassment will do nicely. You won't need great quantities or varieties. Enough wets and drys to fill a modest box will catch just about anything that swims in the backcountry.

Spinning Tackle

Spinning tackle is an easier matter. Nearly every manufacturer markets a lightweight (four- to eight-ounce) open- or closed-face reel, and several makers are offering compact package systems with rods that break into several sections.

The mechanics of getting a spinning lure out are not quite as demanding as casting a flyline, and just about any rod with sufficient backbone will get the job done. Almost any of the multisection backpacking spin rods will do although there are some that seem to cast better than others. Daiwa, a firm that imports cleverly designed spinning and casting tackle, has a line of five-foot, five-piece packing rods for both open- and closed-face reels. These rods come in matched sets with reels and traveling case and cost about $45 for the Minispin open-face system and $30 for the Minicast closed-face outfit. The reels are well designed and crafted to perform their tasks. The carrying cases stash easily anyplace there is fourteen inches of extra space.

A small box of lures including spinners and spoon hardware, small Rapalas, and perhaps a rubber worm or so should round out a balanced backcountry spin kit.

FLY FISHING VS. SPINNING

Although the post-World War II introduction of stationary spool spinning equipment has revolutionized fishing in the United States and made it a sport that nearly one-quarter of the people in the country can participate in, it has not been an unqualified windfall. For one thing, there is a haunting question as to whether our limited and rapidly dwindling fisheries resources can stand the pressure of 50 million well-armed anglers. That pressure on easily accessible waters is probably the main reason you are considering packing into the backcountry to get away from them all.

Truth be known, there is something inherently harmful to fish about spinning. A study conducted in the 1960s by the Michigan Department of Natural Resources clearly indicated that the survival rate of released fish caught on spinning lures and baits was far lower than those released from flies. The multiple-hook arrangements on lures and hardware and the deep-hooking tendency of bait hooks make releasing fish a chancy situation. Releasing fish in the backcountry is equally as important as catching them. As we have already discussed, it is neither an honor nor a boon to stuff your creel with the rare and silly beauties of the wilds. Flies will save those fish the water needs and you really don't want.

There is another argument against spinning that can't be quantified in studies. Fly fishing doesn't give the fisherman an unfair advantage. It doesn't involve the mechanics of whirring gears, the pneumatic push of cams, or other mechanical advantages. It is the simple utilization of a natural force to place a simple lure made of natural materials in a natural place for fish to take it.

This isn't to say that spinning does not have at least a limited place in the backcountry. There are species of game fish, particularly pike, which do not take feathered lures readily. Both large- and smallmouth bass will take fly rod poppers and trout flies at certain times, but can be stubbornly partial to worms and hardware at others.

CLUES TO FISH ACTIVITY

The emphasis in backcountry angling is on simplicity. All you need are a few simple tools and the knowledge to use them. The simplest and easiest to pack piece of angling equipment is observation. Observation and the correct analysis of observed data are critically important to angling anywhere, but in the backcountry they are the first tools you should use, even before you assemble your tackle.

The water always contains clues which indicate what the fish are doing. Watch for flies on the surface of the water, either swimming nymphs near shore or darting fry. They will tell you at what level of the water to seek fish. There are also clues in the weather. If the surface of the water is rippled with a strong breeze, chances are aquatic insects will not be hatching. If it is dimpled with a light rain, put on your poncho and watch for a rise to hatching insects. If it is pouring down, go back to the shelter and stay dry. After the rain ends there could be a feast.

The type of water can also provide hints on what type of fly to use. For instance, a narrow mountain meadow stream is not the best candidate for a large weighted nymph or big streamer fly. Conversely, an immense beaver pond or lake might produce slow action on very tiny dry flies. Match your fly or lure to the water unless there is a good reason to do otherwise.

Backcountry lake fish, particularly alpine lake fish, like to cruise a lot. Food is usually not consistently available in one spot; so they set up dining circuits starting at one point and going around in a routine circle until they return to their original point. If you watch the rises, you can map their circuit and calculate their speed. Normally this circuit is strongly territorial in backcountry water and a pattern of rises almost always indicates a single fish.

After plotting the cruiser's course and estimating his speed, put the fly just ahead of where you think he should be and wait for him to move into it. Remember, your fly need only be an approximation of the natural in most backcountry water.

In rivers or lakes, the dancing of fry or minnows on the surface of the water indicates they are being chased by something they would rather not be caught by. Wakes among the jumping fry are a sure indication that an old cannibal fish is after them and a minnow imitation is in order.

CASTING

Many backcountry lakes and streams pose interesting backcast problems for the wandering fly fisher. One of my favorite lakes is nestled in a bowl between two towering mountains. A backcast can be deftly strung through the brush and trees at the inlet and outlet but the sides of the lake go straight up from a thin rocky mantel. The only way to get a cast out from the sides is to roll it. The roll cast is that graceful-looking but awkward-feeling rod whip which picks up your water-borne line and sends it farther out in a single forward motion. The roll gets me fish

along the sides of this lake and in many other backcountry waters
I fish. It is often the only way of getting a fly out.

FISHING ATTIRE

I can't imagine anybody hauling hip boots or waders up miles
of brushy or rocky trails to keep their pants dry while fishing
backcountry water. During the summer it is usually warm
enough during the day to wade in shorts and tennis shoes; and if
it isn't, you can always do your casting from rocks or hummocks
around the shore.

BEST FISHING HOURS

In the summer, lowland fishing is normally restricted to dawn
and dusk, when the surface temperature is cool enough for fish
and insects to move around comfortably. In shaded backcountry
streams and alpine lakes surface temperatures do not vary that
much, and fish and insects cannot really afford to siesta all day.
Hatching and feeding activity is often an all-day affair and may
go nonstop for days and nights on end.

A friend of mine camped with me on an upland meadow stream
a few years ago for a couple of days. We fished through the first
afternoon and evening, caught several chunky smallish cutthroats, and crawled into our bags that night content. We were
camped not ten feet from the stream, and during the night I
awoke several times to a symphony of splashing. Before
breakfast the next morning I walked up the creek to see if I could
find out what all the excitement was about.

I found it. There were shoals literally three feet deep of spent
gray drakes stacked up against every snag in the river. The spinners had fallen during the night and the fish had dined and
danced until dawn.

We fished and napped that day, again catching a few young
friskies. But we stayed up that night for the main event. About
midnight the feeding began and lasted until we were too groggy
to notice. Each of us landed a sixteen-inch cutthroat (very large
for that stream) and lost several others to snags during the nocturnal frenzy.

COOKING FISH

To some people cooking an evening fish by waterside means frying it in sizzling butter over campfire coals. To them I say haul in your fry pan and greasy butter (which has a way of working its way around the pack on the way up) and *bon appetit*.

Let me suggest another way of cooking fish worthy your palate and the backcountry mood which is as ripe with pagan frivolity as a respectable person would want to indulge.

Every fall there is a lake trout festival on the Keweenaw Peninsula of northern Michigan. The Finnish stock people who throw the fling spend a couple of days fishing the bays and shores of Lake Superior for enough of the husky trout to sate the appetites of the community and guests.

On the afternoon of the feast they build bonfires along the coast of the lake and prepare a heavy egg-floating brine in large iron kettles. As evening approaches and the celebrants become restive for dinner, the fish are skewered lengthwise on stakes, dipped in the brine and staked directly over the fire. When the brine burns off, the fish is dipped again and the process repeated until the meat is flaky and succulent. I have never had better-tasting fish anywhere and have since taken a leaf from their cookbook on all my backcountry fishing excursions.

The recipe requires only a jigger of salt, a pot (one pint is large enough for most of the fish I catch) large enough to hold the brine, a willow stake, and a modest fire. The only problem you are likely to encounter with small fish is the flesh falling away from the skewer during the broiling or brining. This is easy to prevent by running a second skewer over the fish's spine and tying the two skewers together at either end of the fish.

The ingredients of the recipe are not nearly as awkward or messy to carry as conventional frying paraphernalia and I feel it is certainly a nobler way for a wild trout to go than in a fry pan identical to the last resting place of a lowland fish.

Fish are an excellent source of protein but do not really constitute a well-balanced meal. A fish broil (or fry if you still insist) should be complemented with green vegetables and carbohydrates (instant potatoes or the like). This not only makes for a healthier, better-balanced meal but also saves excessive wear and tear on limited backcountry fish populations. It would require the lives of two ten- to twelve-inch fish to sate a trail-hungry hiker without other food, but as an entree, one fish combined with nourishing packed-in foods will make a satisfying meal.

KEEPING WILDLIFE FREELOADERS AWAY

The backcountry has odd ways of suspending what we have come to think of as natural laws. For instance, in our sheltered conceit, we have come to think that if you keep a fish reasonably cool, it will keep overnight and even for a day or two. In the wilds, the opposite is true. Fish almost surely will not last overnight even in the fresh, cool mountain air. Attempting to keep them could easily be dangerous to your health.

The reason for this apparent biological paradox is not some rare form of bacteria that thrives only in the wilds; rather it is the habit backcountry carnivorous and scavenging animals have of looking around for tasty, convenient midnight snacks. Depending on the woodland critter that is raiding your fridge, the encounter can range from the minor inconvenience of a partially eaten breakfast fish left by a mouse or jay, to the major annoyance of a skunk, to outright mayhem or murder by a bear. It is far healthier to just keep what you are going to eat at the next meal because whatever you try to stash won't keep anyway.

Midnight marauders can be attracted by less than a whole fish. Entrails or even dirty dishes left about are enough to attract their attention. Clean your fish away from camp, leaving entrails on the shore (where they will get eaten quicker than if you leave them in the water), and be scrupulously fastidious about garbage around camp. Wash fishy dishes immediately after dinner and pour the dishwater into a hole where it can be buried.

GUARDING YOUR FISHING FINDS

The worst thing that can happen to that secluded backcountry pond with all the dumb and lovely fish you found last year is to have somebody build a road to it. The second worst is to have somebody, including yourself, build a trail. Unselfish sharing is one of the characteristics that mark good breeding, but there are limits to even the best of goodfellowhood. Although many people share their homes and bank accounts, few will share their spouse or pipe and I have never yet met a fisherperson who would knowingly reveal the whereabouts of his favorite secret hole to any but his closest chums.

It sometimes requires a high refinement of guile and counter-espionage to keep the location of a good spot confidential. Robert Traver in his books *Trout Madness* and *The Anatomy of a Fisherman* studied the state of the art of fishing hole security in Michigan's Upper Peninsula. I worked and fished with these sylvan folks for two years and discovered an entire underground of intelligence and counterintelligence directed respectively at discovering other people's favorite hunting and fishing grounds and concealing their own. I was spied upon and, after two years, noticed that I began paying attention to which direction my fellow sportsmen were going. I never actually followed anybody (which is not considered unethical in the U.P.) but did stoop to following up on leads.

I also learned to become cunning in covering my tracks. A really good spot which would have been worth a lot on the secret hole black market, such as the beaver pond we talked about earlier, was worth extreme precautions.

My friend and I seldom took the same route to the pond to avoid making a trail. Sometimes we would drive a few miles out of our way and then double back carefully, hiding the car before jumping off into the bush. If we suspected there were others about, we would even take the precaution of dusting over our tire tracks and covering footprints left in the mud.

Actually, looking back on my paranoid days in the U.P., where looking over your shoulder was as important to good fishing as a neat cast, I think perhaps surreptitiousness actually adds something to the sport. After all, what is the fun of having a secret hole if you can't have fun keeping it secret?

CHAPTER 6

Backcountry Big Game

Churning deep within the most fundamental chemistry of our bodies is this strange thing, this drive, that makes us stop whatever civilized task we are doing in real life and go out into an alien land to kill beasts for food.

It is buried so deep within our makeup it cannot be identified or labeled and yet is undeniably there. It is a link in our genetic train that has survived the atrophy of collective civilization since man first picked up a tool and used it to gather his food.

Many, however, see this drive as anathema—a lingering piece of body baggage that had a function at one time, like the appendix, but is now more a nuisance. They argue that another part of our basic makeup has developed the means which enable humans to avoid subjecting themselves to the dangers, stresses, and paradoxes of the field and mountain to forage for food. They point to the complicated and efficient system of food growing, processing, and delivery that civilization has evolved and insist that it is absurd and probably immoral for humans to continue acting like Neanderthals chasing innocent creatures through the wilds.

They do have a point. For most of the estimated 25 million Americans who hunt, the entire process of hunting—from the expense of outfitting to the time off work spent in the fields for a chance at a game animal—is unquestionably a negative economic proposition. Taking a week off to hunt probably costs the average worker in the area of $250 in lost earnings. On top of this are the costs of the trip, which average at least $100 and as much as $1,000, all things considered. Figuring in amortization of hunting equipment, rifle, bullets, clothing and gear, the sum probably comes to about $50 per animal for a good hunter. Add everything up and fifty pounds of deer meat probably has an average individual cost of about $500. That is $10 a pound and you can buy a pretty nice cut of prime beef for that kind of money.

But there is something about hunting that a prime filet mignon bought at the butcher shop is not going to satisfy, and that is why we hunt in spite of the costs, dangers, and bother. That is why the people who only see the economics of hunting and their own thin moral reasoning are missing something basic to human existence.

The twentieth-century Spanish philosopher Ortega y Gasset felt that hunting was the basic relationship between human beings and the land and that practicing hunting was an existential gesture between the individual and his alienated environment. He says, "Thus the principle which inspires hunting for sport is that of artificially perpetuating, as a possibility for man, a situation which is archaic in the highest degree: that early state in which, already human, he still lived within the orbit of animal existence." For Ortega, then, hunting was a kind of reaffirmation of the human kinship to animals.

Ernest Hemingway, the American literary he-man, also saw the relationship between hunter and hunted as an existential one. Hemingway saw the metaphysical joining of one man and one animal in a momentary event. For him, this ephemeral relationship was a contest between two heroic, sapient creatures, each with a motive and each with something to prove. The winner of the contest, in Hemingway stories such as *The Short Happy Life of Francis Macomber,* was the better man or beast. It is an equal contest of wills.

Novelist Tom McGuane feels, like Ortega, that our relationship to game animals has not changed in the million years we have been using tools. It is simply an honorable way to feed oneself. In an article in *Outside Magazine* he wrote: "Nobody who loves to hunt feels absolutely hunky-dory when the quarry goes down . . . the remorse spins out almost before anything and the balancing act ends on one declination or another. I decided that unless I become a vegetarian, I'll get my meat by hunting for it. I feel absolutely unabashed by arguments of other carnivores who get their meat in plastic with blue numbers on it."

Hunting does not require justification. It is an important part of how we grew up as a species and is part of our relationship with our environment. No matter how complex or efficient our social organizations become, we will always remain basically a hunting animal.

HUNTING ETHICS

That does not mean there are no holds barred in our quest for quarry or that any way we can kill game is fair under the ground rules set in our existential makeup. Few people would consider dropping bombs from airplanes an appropriate or sporting way of filling tags, and machine guns are not only illegal but universally considered unethical. Jacklighting, using a bright light to freeze game at night, traps, and snares are also against the law and commonly frowned upon.

These methods are illegal and unethical. We call people who use them poachers, poor sportsmen, game hogs, and worse. However, we tend to venerate the person who kills one of the handful of grizzly bears still existing in the lower United States, knowing he left the meat to rot where it fell. Somehow we admire the rug or mounted head of this wasted animal and justify the achievement as "man's noble legacy as a hunting animal."

We hunters have managed to refine a rather restrictive ethic on the acceptable methods of hunting but have somehow lost sight of a motivational ethic: a set of rules governing why we hunt and, consequently, what we should hunt.

All creatures kill to survive. It is the way nature works and ultimately a healthy way of operating the world. Few creatures ever kill more than they can eat or things they do not intend to eat. A skunk may blindly slash its way through a chicken coop or an otter through a salmon pool, but these are exceptions to the normal behavior of hunting animals and are usually given much opprobrium by us sporting folk. We acknowledge that killing to eat is the mechanics of nature, but wanton bloodshed is abhorred by all of nature.

So why do otherwise perfectly respectable hunters kill bears they wouldn't think of eating? Why do others shoot mountain goats or sheep and leave all but the head rotting on the rocks? Are we subject to the same aberrant bloodlust as the skunk and the otter?

Hunting has always been and should remain basically a way of getting food. Killing animals for food, along with fishing and plant gathering, is the way human beings fueled their evolution. Food is still the only valid reason for taking the life of a fellow creature. Killing for a head, a hide, a tusk, or a stuffed caricature of the animal is a perversion of the human hunting reflex.

Every year thousands of magnificent animals are wasted because we haven't been able to figure out why we hunt. The worst of it is that our "shoot anything that moves" ethic is endangering whole species.

Since moving to the North American continent, Europeans have managed to reduce the number of wild species here by some score. We are now in the process of pushing several other species to the brink of extinction. Many animals are backed up against the wall by the inexorable pressure of the miner, the forester, and the real estate agent. Although these economic pressures have put many species on the brink of extinction, it may be hunters who push them over.

The grizzly bear, a handy example, at one time inhabited most of the United States west of the Mississippi and ranged well into the Midwest. Today it is caught in a narrow belt of mountains between Yellowstone and Glacier national parks. Biologists estimate there are no more than a few hundred individuals left and possibly considerably fewer (the vast territorial demands of adults and the rugged country they now inhabit make it difficult to make an accurate census). The U.S. Fish and Wildlife Service has declared the grizzly a threatened species and placed his welfare under modest federal control. However, the animal is still hunted on a quota basis in Montana by sportsmen and without restriction by Indians on two reservations.

The problem for the bear is a little trick biologists call "minimal numbers." This means the bear's range is strictly limited and its numbers, in turn, restricted to the quantity of suitable habitat within that finite range. There probably will never be more grizzly bears in the lower states than there are today and sooner or later some cyclical phenomenon, natural disaster, or disease will reduce the population to a tenuous threshold level during which the death of one breeding adult could spell the end of the species.

It is conceivable, and probably inevitable unless the bear is protected, that a hunter will someday figuratively kill the last of the species.

I don't think anyone would want to live with the distinction of being responsible for the destruction not just of an individual but of an entire breeding population of animals. Hunters, especially backcountry hunters, who follow their sport in the same environment inhabited by threatened species, are going to have to redefine the meaning of game animal to avoid fundamental conflicts of conscience. A game animal should have value as a source of food, be plentiful enough to assure that hunting is not going to harm local populations, and have enough sporting qualities to make hunting interesting.

In the lower forty-eight states this pretty much reduces the catalog of quarry to whitetail deer, mule deer and, in some areas, elk and moose. Within their very limited range the pronghorn antelope may also qualify, but for the purpose of this chapter we will only consider the first four.

The deer, particularly the whitetail, fits our definition of game like a buckskin glove. It is not only good-tasting when properly cared for and famously sporting, there is ample evidence that hunting actually assures the health and well-being of deer populations. With deer, hunters can have their cake and eat it too.

Deer are the cosmopolitan game animals of North America, found just about everywhere from the deepest wilderness to the backyards of the suburbs. They thrive under nearly any conditions, and the only problem they encounter in certain environments is overstressing their supply of winter feed.

Not so, however, with elk and moose. Both have specific demands in habitat and neither will truck much variety or pressure. The once extensive range of the two animals has shriveled to remote areas in a few underdeveloped states and continues to shrink under heavy economic pressures.

Both elk and moose can tolerate some proximity to human agencies during most of the year, although they seem to prefer keeping their distance. However, in the early spring when the winter stresses have put them on the edge of existence and the cows are ready to calve, they need absolute security. During this time they usually seek low, heavy cover such as foothill pine stands for elk and heavy brambles in marshy areas for moose. Consequently, the density of any elk or moose population is strictly limited to the quantity and quality of these environmental elements.

Unfortunately for elk, moose, and us, these are the very areas of wild country that are currently attracting the greatest economic interest. In the West foresters are starting to exploit these foothill stands of timber for their commercial value, cattlemen are extending their spring grazing range into the heavily covered hills, and snowmobilers and other springtime recreationists are penetrating the elk's maternity wards.

In the East, residential and agricultural interests are moving into the sanctuary of moose and driving them into less ideal calving yards.

Some biologists feel that habitat disruptions are driving both animals into the same minimal numbers situation as the grizzly bear. Within the very near future, according to these specialists, the limitations of suitable range will reduce the populations of both to the point where they would not be able to recover from extensive random mortalities.

Most states that still have populations of elk and moose continue to allow hunting, sometimes on a limited basis. The question of how much economic and hunting pressure these animals can take before they become locked into an inexorable decline is something every backcountry hunter is going to have to deal with.

If you still insist on hunting these beleaguered animals, there is only one way of avoiding a conflict of the hunter's conscience. You must spend at least as much time and money protecting the habitat of these creatures as you spend hunting them. This means donating to, and getting involved with, local conservation groups to lobby for the preservation of critical habitat, opposing the economic development of areas within their range, and seeing to it that calving yards are spared the pressures of snowmobilers and spring cattle grazing. It isn't as easy and painless as it sounds. You will be fighting bureaucrats and businessmen and will probably be in open conflict with people formerly regarded as friends. That is the price you are going to have to pay for your bacon.

STALK PACKING

As I pointed out at the beginning of this chapter, the only thing about backcountry hunting that differs from stalking in the lowlands is the fact that you will be carrying your camp while you hunt, nomad style.

There are backcountry hunters who sacrifice the possibility of seeing game on the way into and out of a camp by clambering and clanking over rough trails with burgeoning packs. They establish a protracted backcountry camp, hunt out of that for a few days, then pack everything up and haul it out, along with whatever booty they have managed to pick up, on an equally arduous return trip.

The advantages of this system are the added creature comforts you can haul along and the security of a well-defined camp. However, if you pack light, the thirty to thirty-five pounds we talked about in chapter 1, and use one of the new generation self-forming soft packs which carry without much more effort than your shirt, you can be hunting the moment you leave the trailhead.

Big Game Hunting Pack

Lightweight frameless pack (a Compac 2 by Maran) with the following gear: down fall-winter sleeping bag, wool handsocks, wool mittens, fanny pack, rope, sleeping pad, poncho, sweatshirt, wool sweater, blaze orange down jacket, down booties, two extra pairs of wool socks, bivouac cover for sleeping bag, food bag, stove and fuel, cook set, hunting knife, Swiss Army knife, binoculars, toilet paper, orange-topped wool Balaclava cap, and extra pants. On your belt carry ammo pouch and canteen with rifle over your shoulder.

Gear for Back and Belt

Everything you really need for three to four days of a moving feast can be stashed in a carefully packed medium-weight pack. Enough freeze-dried and trail foods for four days have a dry weight of from two to four pounds; add another two pounds for a light stove to cook them. A shelter tarp for two weighs another two pounds. The sleeping bag is a heavyweight at four pounds. A waterproof poncho (which doubles as a sleeping groundcloth) adds another six ounces. For the foam pad, add another pound; compass and map, about four ounces; rope (100 feet of quarter-inch nylon), about two pounds; a pair of tennis shoes or down booties (depending on the weather) for loafing, about a pound; down jacket or vest (again depending on weather) and extra clothing, two to four pounds; a lightweight rifle and ammunition, about eight pounds. That list, the things that will go in your pack or across your shoulders, will weigh from twenty-eight to thirty pounds. This gives you easily enough tolerance to add a pair of binoculars (from six ounces to a pound), a small camera (about a pound and one-half), and a notebook and pencil, which will tack on an additional two and one-half pounds. Add the two pounds for the pack and our back load is thirty-two to thirty-four pounds, which is as close to being between thirty and thirty-five pounds as you can get.

On your belt carry a folding lock-blade knife, a GI canteen with cup (for boiling water), and a folding pocket pouch for quick ammunition. All of this weight, about four pounds with the canteen full, will neither pull on the same muscles and joints as your back burden nor conflict with easy, graceful travel through the country.

The canteen should be taped so that it doesn't rattle inside the cup. The easiest way of doing this is to tape crosses on the bottom of the canteen with cotton bandage and make a couple of wraps around the canteen where the lip of the cup touches. You might also tape the cup handle to keep it from scraping and to protect your hand while you are cooking.

Stalking Technique

That is everything you need for a nomad stalk. All you have to remember while you are on the move is that you are stalking or still-hunting and not hiking. This means cutting back your ranger forced-march pace to a crawl.

Walk a few paces at a time, stop, look around and listen, then a few more paces. Work your way into the country, not only physically but mentally. Attempt to become a part of the environment. Stop thinking of yourself as a human being in an alien place and think of yourself as an animal who has come home.

Use your best senses, which are your eyes and ears. Let them guide you to the places your quarry is most likely to be. Let your senses become part of the landscape and they will be more able to penetrate it.

Wild animals lie down wherever they find themselves when they tire and so does the nomadic hunter. There are no destinations; so anyplace that is suitable when dusk begins to fall is the right place. However, some places are righter than others. Water in a nomadic bivouac is advantageous (although you can carry enough for dinner), and so is a spot which will provide an opportunity to see game at dusk and dawn.

Heavily used trails got that way because game found them convenient for their regular itinerary. Common watering holes are especially good campsites because animals usually like to have a sip before they go off on the night's business and before they retire in the early morning. Pick a spot with a good view of the waterhole but at some distance. Check the prevailing wind to make sure you are downwind from the hole and set up a low-profile, quiet bivouac. Keep the stove fire low while fixing dinner (or wait until after dark to eat), and keep an eye on the hole and its approaches. You will see motion before you see game and you will see the animals before you hear them.

After shooting hours, which in most states end at sundown or half an hour after, don't throw a party. Remain as quiet as possible all night (snores should be the loudest noise from the bivouac) because game moving by your spot after dark will remember you are there if they detect you and will avoid the place in the morning.

Hunting with your dominant senses, telling them what you are looking for and allowing them to lead the way with as little interference from your head as possible, is not only productive, it is fun. You will be amazed at the variety of sensual pleasures that

Nomad Stalking on Skis

abound in the backcountry if you don't monitor everything through your conscious mind and allow yourself to lapse into thought or day-dreaming. Keep your senses alert. Know what they are up to but just take note of it; don't try to influence them.

One of the things your conscious mind can be doing while it is being led about the wilderness by your senses is to minimize your chances of alarming the quarry. Most game animals smell and hear better than they see. So, as much as possible, keep the breeze in your face while you are traveling. If this doesn't work out, try to quarter it or work at right angles to it and direct your senses to the upwind side. Be aware of every step you take; know where it is going and what is under it. Think quiet and walk quiet. Walk at a pace you can maintain without breathing too heavily and when you stop, stop dead. Watch for motion or the stopping of motion around you. It is your senses against the game's and, at least in this respect, they have most of the cards; so you are going to have to try harder.

Keeping Track of Your Whereabouts

Another routine but important task your mind can be doing while all of this is going through your senses is to keep track of yourself. You are allowing your unpredictable senses to lead you along the erratic tracks of a wild animal who is always at home. If you want to find your way back, you are going to have to know where you are. Keep your direction in the back of your mind. When you change directions, know how much in which direction and how it will affect your bearings. Check your compass every few times you stop. If you are in an area with mountains or other prominent land features, you can run an occasional triangulation to find your location. If you know you are following a stream watershed, you won't have much to worry about, but just remember how you got there.

Several years ago in Michigan I was nomad stalking up a stream which flowed quickly from a run of rolling forested hills. My eyes were following a trail of a big whitetail as it meandered along the drainage of the creek. At one point near the top of a set of hills, he stopped at a marshy area to drink, then waded the stream and poked off to the right. I followed, confident I could backtrack to the stream and easily find my way back.

About a mile later I found him lying down in a thick copse of trees. I was downwind of him, and we sensed each other about the same time. I was standing and ready and he had to get up; so I had the fatal advantage.

I cleaned and hung him, and since it was getting late, decided to spend the night there. I got a cozy little bivouac set up just as it started to snow heavily, built a fire (I didn't have a stove in those days), and snuggled in for a cozy night in my bag.

The next morning I broke camp, took the deer in tow, and charted a course back to the creek somewhat downstream of where I had left it in an attempt to save a half mile or so of rough timber.

The skidding was downhill and over fresh snow; so it was easy. I was humming along when suddenly I realized that this wasn't my stream. It was the right size and ran through the right kind of terrain, but it wasn't the one I had hunted up. I had already logged five or six miles downhill, which was most of the way back to my car—or was it? I pulled out the map and gasped as I discovered two thin blue lines running downhill from a patch of blue hummocks. The marsh where my deer had stopped to drink was the headwater of both my stream and another. When I had crossed over after him I had also crossed what I thought was a channel to my stream. But the channel matured into another stream upon which I now found myself dumbfounded and embarrassingly misplaced.

From where I was, it would have required a two- or three-mile hike over a fairly high ridge and through a lot of wicked-looking brush to get back to the original stream. On the other hand, the stream I was on would reach a road in about six miles and would put me about eight road miles from my car. I decided to take my chances on the present course and finished off the day in sight of the road. I camped there and broke out the next morning after carefully concealing my deer in a thicket above the stream. About halfway to the car I got a ride and was back to my deer before noon; so the story has a happy ending. My happiness was tempered with the realization that I should not have taken so much for granted in the backcountry and should not have neglected to consult my map before changing my directions.

WEAPONS

Fair means for taking big game means either a high-powered rifle or a bow and arrow. However, in many western states big-bore pistols have become a chic way of proving bold daring. I have heard of people even going after grizzly with .44 Magnum pistols, which indicates more stupidity than courage. It is true that pistols are lighter and more compact than other hunting weapons, and there is no doubt about their sufficiency of power at close range. The problem is that very few people can hold them steadily enough to shoot much over thirty-five or forty yards and expect a clean kill.

Rifles

Rifles are undoubtedly the most efficient game weapon although they do not have the macho appeal of a big pistol or the challenge of a bow and arrow. They get the job done quickly and well and, if you don't go overboard for gadgets and power, are not unreasonably burdensome to carry.

Most people who have bothered so far with this book will already have a hunting rifle. In all probability, it will at least suffice for the tasks in the backcountry. The only qualifications for a suitable pack rifle is that it be of appropriately powerful caliber, from 6 mm on up, and not weigh enough to make it unpleasant to carry. Within those liberal parameters, just about anything goes.

Shooting conditions, of course, should be kept in mind. For instance, a .243 is probably not going to hack it in the bush of a northeastern whitetail marsh. Heavy cover is the place for larger, more pockey bullets which can whittle a lot of brush before they are detoured. On the other hand, a .35 Remington, ideal in the brush, would be less than ideal for open mountain country, where shots are usually long and a flat trajectory is used.

A .460 Weatherby is a lot more bullet than is needed for a 250-pound deer. So, for that matter, is the 7 mm Remington

Magnum. And these big, powerful cartridges are normally, by necessity, housed in large, long, and heavy rifles.

So, although just about any rifle will do, some will do a lot better than others for backcountry hunting, and some calibers perform better in certain terrains than others.

There is probably no single ideal hunting rifle for all situations or for all people, and this rule certainly applies to backcountry rifles. The best compromise packing rifle for all occasions would have a substantial .30 caliber bullet, a relatively light recoil, and reasonably flat trajectory; it would be lightweight, short, accurate, and reliable. In calibers, this probably can be reduced to cartridges in the class of the .308 Winchester and 7 mm Mauser. Both of these cartridges hold their respectable muzzle velocity very well over midrange, each moving a 180-grain bullet at about 1,900 feet per second at 200 yards. Both pack sufficient midrange energy, 1,400 pounds and 1,500 pounds respectively. They both hold a remarkably flat flight at 200 yards, dropping only about 3.5 inches. Best of all, neither of them will put any permanent dents in your shoulder, and both are famous for being more accurate than they should be.

The backcountry rifle should also be as short and light as possible, or practical. Short barrels are an anathema to some people because they shave a bit off cartridge ballistics (very little, twenty-five to fifty feet per second muzzle velocity for each inch less than twenty-two inches) and generate an annoying report. In backpack rifles, I feel both of these drawbacks are worthwhile trade-offs for the packing convenience and quickness of a short barrel. I like a lightweight eighteen-inch barrel but up to twenty still makes a sweet, compact weapon.

Because reliability is so important when you are a long way from a gunsmith, a backcountry rifle should be based on the simplest and most robust action available. This simply means a bolt-action magazine rifle of the Mauser type such as military Mausers, Springfields, Eddystone Enfields, Winchester Model 70, Remington 700, or Savage 110. Hunters who swear by slide-and-lever actions probably know all of their eccentricities and how to deal with them. The rest of us are better off with the bolt because there is so little that can go wrong with it.

Automatics are normally heavy and bulky and always more

Backcountry Rifles

At left is a lightweight restocked and scoped .308 Winchester on a military Mauser 98 action. A simpler version on the right is a chopped .303 British Enfield which shoots well and costs practically nothing. Both rifles have short eighteen-inch barrels for easier maneuvering in tight cover and rocks.

Hunter Drawing a Bead on Elk in the Bob Marshall Wilderness
(Photo by Harley Hettick)

prone to malfunction than simpler mechanisms. Single-shots, which should have disappeared from the market a century ago, have stubbornly held on during the past century and are even becoming a sort of cult weapon today. People who use them seem to think they are more sporting than repeaters, or more accurate. Either way I think they are splitting hairs. The value of a quick second shot is the elimination of unnecessary suffering of a wounded animal and tiresome miles of tracking a blood spoor.

The only American firms making short-barreled bolt-action car-bines today are Remington, with an eighteen-inch Model 600 Mohawk, and Savage with a carbine twenty-inch barrel version of the 110. Several importing firms handle European carbines, including the Mannlicher-Schoonhower and Styer Mannlicher, but they are unreasonably expensive—$500 compared to the $150 to $200 for either of the American-made carbines.

Rifle Scopes and Sights

There is still a debate over rifle scopes even though they have
been around nearly half a century and have been developed to the
point where they are tough, accurate, reliable, and weatherproof.
Some people feel more comfortable with open sights, particularly
receiver peeps, because they feel such sights are less likely to be
jarred out of alignment and offer a better quick-pointing bead
than scopes. No doubt they are right about the ruggedness of iron
sights. They present very little profile to be knocked around and,
even if they should take a hard crack, are stout enough to hold
their bead.

However, I feel that modern scopes are actually quicker than
any design of iron sight because they isolate the target in a magnified image. The new duplex cross hairs, with their heavy bars
stepping down from the side of the image into fine cross hairs in
the middle, provide both a quick sight reference and a precision
bead.

My eyes never were as keen as they used to be, and the little bit
of magnification I get through a scope (I prefer only a little bit)
gives me the edge I did not come equipped with. I like my shots
close, 100 yards being the farthest I feel comfortable with, and I
would rather try sneaking in closer than risk a shot much longer.
I normally use a three-power scope, which brings my 100-yard
target up to about 30 yards, where I can be a little choosy about
picking the right spot.

However, I wouldn't go hunting into the backcountry without
a little hedge on my bets. My pack rifle is equipped with both a
scope and iron sights. The rifle has a bead front sight, and I had a
gunsmith mount a flip-up peep on the rear scope mount, which is
fixed at a fifty-yard sight-in. If something should happen to my
scope, I merely take if off, flip up the rear peep, and am back in
business.

Barrel Shortening

My rifle is a Mexican short-model Mauser 98, which handles
the .308 Winchester smoothly without any wasted metal. I had
the barrel trimmed to eighteen inches, which made the gunsmith

cringe because it was a fairly rare John Buhmiller blank. But the extra four inches would probably have served more as a leaf rake and rock banger than a means for greater accuracy. I spent some spare time one winter making a full-length Mannlicher stock for it which isn't especially fancy but does protect the barrel and allows me to anchor my sling farther up the barrel.

The overall length of my gun is just thirty-eight inches, with thirty-two of them covered by the sling. This means that when I carry it on my back only six inches protrude either over my shoulder or around my butt. The gun takes up exactly as much space as my stooping or bending trunk. If I clear an obstacle, so will my gun.

I swapped for the basic unit—the action and barrel— a couple of years ago at a value of about $40. The stock from Herters cost me another $25, and the scope is a Bushnell Scope Chief I picked up on sale for $35. The folding peep is made by Redfield (to fit their mounts) and cost me $5 to have it mounted on mine. The gunsmith also got $12 for shortening the barrel and remounting the front sight. He added a set of obsolete mounts and drilled and tapped them for $10. My total cash investment was $122 and that, with a little foul-weather work on the stock, provided me with a tidy, handy pack rifle weighing just eight pounds with all of its frills and anxiety pacifiers.

Whittling down a Mauser or some other veteran of ancient wars is an inexpensive way, if you don't value your time too highly, of getting into a packing rifle. All that is really required, if you are not sensitive about the figure you cut, is shortening the barrel (which should be done by a gunsmith unless you know how to operate a lathe and how to reheadspace the barrel), mounting it with sights, and grinding off some of the superfluous metal and wood. A graceful new stock is nice but the one it was issued with will do. Just trim it up a bit to take the military square corners off.

Military Rifles

Although full-dress military rifles have now been elevated to the status of collectors' items, short-stocked ordnance and somebody else's attempts at sporterizing are still bargains, usually only a fraction of what a new or even used commercial rifle would cost. The British Enfield, one of the last of the really great bargains, is a much better rifle than most people give it credit for in its native .303 caliber and can still be bought in decent condition for $25 to $40. The more desirable Mausers, Springfields, and Eddystone Enfields in military 8 mm and .30-06 generally fetch about double the money, from $50 to $75, mostly because the actions are more versatile and the rifles convert to somewhat cleaner-looking sporters.

Bows

Bowhunters may be the last of the romantic idealists. They take their primitive weapons afield, seeking not only game but also some kind of heroic ideal—a moment when their primitive weapon will serve as a catalyst for a rare form of reality. Bowhunters are obviously not in it just for the meat; some practice their sport for a higher satisfaction of vanity, others for beauty and truth.

For those who are motivated by the latter, there is surely no better place to find the possibility of either than the backcountry. Game is less cautious away from the realms of civilization and more likely to accommodate bowhunters with the close, steady shots they need. The simplicity of archery seems to fit into the splendor of the wilds. If truth and beauty exist at all, the backcountry is probably the only place you will find them.

Modern archery equipment has taken two diverse courses in development. The ancient, simple compression bow has undergone sane, rational development since it was resurrected from oblivion about fifty years ago. This trend is currently represented by short, light, powerful recurve glass and wood laminated bows which are far better than the deadly horn bows of Ghengis Khan, better than the accurate longbows of the English yeomen at Cressy, better in fact, than any bow in history.

Not long ago, tournament archers developed compound bows that don't rely on simple compression of the bow stock for power but use a system of pulleys to produce the energy to drive the arrow. Compound bows develop enormous energy smoothly through the pulleys and require only minimal effort to draw.

Many hunters have begun using them in preference to more traditional bows because the leverage offered by the pulleys multiplies the drawing power of the string as much as 50 percent. The pulleys on compound bows can also be adjusted to produce more or less power as the situation demands.

However, compounds are heavy, bulky, have an annoying way of attracting twigs, leaves, and branches, and are not as easy to maneuver in tight cover. Their power makes them ideal weapons on the target line or in hunting areas where their complicated mechanism is not a liability. In the backcountry, where a low packing profile is absolutely necessary, they are out of place.

The same rules that apply to pack rifles should also be reflected in the choice of a backcountry bow. It should be powerful enough to do the job, yet light and compact. In terms of what is available today, this means one of the short "magnum" wood and glass composite recurves. It should have as much power as you can draw comfortably—forty to fifty pounds is ideal—and either be short enough to fit snugly around your back or break down into a packable package.

Breakdown bows, of course, have the disadvantage of being broken down when you run into game on the way in or out of the backcountry. On the other hand, even short forty-nine-inch one-piece magnum bows tend to stick out from your body and catch much of what your body is able to dodge.

The short bow has trade-offs compared to longer weapons. One mechanical disadvantage of the short bow is its magnification of sighting error, which will pull an arrow farther off course than will a longer one. Short bows also tend to stack; that is, they require much more strength to pull the string back to anchor than longer bows which can distribute compression over a greater length. If you are going to use one of the short hunters, and most people I know who pack bows do, make sure you know how to use it and what your maximum range is. Twenty-five yards is about the greatest distance at which most short bow hunters can manage to place a killing arrow with any assurance.

Arrows

Arrows are a matter of personal choice but make sure they fit both your draw length and your bow's draw and power. Aluminum shafts with one of the many four-surface broadhead points are generally preferred because they penetrate deeply and the shafts tend to bend rather than break, allowing the cutting edges of the point to do more damage inside the wound and kill quicker.

Bow quivers are fast and convenient and most bowhunters prefer them. A four-arrow bow quiver that has a point-protecting cup is sufficient for packing; you can strap four more shafts on your pack with points removed and stored someplace in or on your pack.

HABITS OF GAME ANIMALS

Game animals, like all other living creatures, need food, water, and a cozy place to live. Knowledge of the way a species meets these basic needs is the most important tool any hunter can take into the field. However, as anybody who has hunted can attest, all game animals have many devices to offset their vulnerability while meeting these needs. The trick to hunting is to use their needs-satisfying habits while avoiding their natural strengths.

Whitetail Deer

The whitetail deer (*Odocoileus virginianus*) is often regarded as the most astute of North America's big game species. Although I hesitate to use an anthropomorphic term like astute to characterize a nonhuman species, the word came naturally to my typewriter and I think I will leave it because whitetail have a spooky way of using humanlike intelligence to foil their most dangerous predator.

The whitetail is found just about everywhere in North America in a dozen different subspecies ranging from the pocket-sized Key deer of Florida to the 200-pound flagtail of the northern tier of states. Its wide distribution and tolerance of (and in some cases, preference for) humans and their doings may have contributed to its celebrated sagacity. However, its natural way of dealing with the dangers of its preferred habitat probably has more to do with it.

Whitetail Buck
(Drawing by Tony M. Sandoval)

Whitetails are the deer of heavy cover, dense woodlands, brush, and high grass. When they feel threatened, they can disappear into this impenetrable curtain in a flashing whisper. Danger can make them change their daily habits from diurnal to strictly nocturnal.

Their acute sense of threat is keyed to several early warning systems provided to them by evolution. They rely most heavily on their extremely sensitive olfactory organs. In the right situation, they can smell and identify a hunter or other predator more than a mile away and will always smell a human long before a human can see them if the breeze is in their nose. A biologist friend of mine feels that the deer's nose so dominates its behavior that its entire conception of the world is translated in scent images rather than the visual landscape pictures we have.

The whitetail's ears are also extremely sensitive, many times more so than ours, and almost as reliable as its nose in detecting danger. The habit whitetails have of working their head around a 300-degree arc from one flank to another is calculated to permit their scoop-shaped ears to pick up the faintest crackle hundreds of yards away. The forest and bush they live in are a constant source of extraneous noise and they can't afford to be startled or even alerted to all of it. Only noise that represents a threat, such as the even gait of a hunter, triggers a defense mechanism.

Although a whitetail's vision is not its keenest sense (deer are color blind and see only disconcerted images on both sides of their head), its eyes are extremely sensitive to minute motion. A whitetail can spot the blink of an eye hundreds of feet away and react instantly to the movement of an arm 100 yards away.

Throughout most of its range the whitetail is a home-loving creature, seldom moving beyond one or two square miles throughout its normal six- to eight-year lifespan. It will migrate if forced to by weather, food, or hunting pressure but will usually return to its turf as soon as possible. Berries, shoots, seeds, nuts, and leaves are its favorite cuisine in the backcountry; but it can eat any plant substance from grass to bark if it has to.

Mule Deer

The mule deer (*Odocoileus hemionus*) is the deer of the mountains and plateaus of the West. It has a reputation of being relatively dumb compared to the whitetail but, of course, that is silly. The muley, or blacktail as it is often called in the West, merely has a different way of relating to danger in his more sparsely vegetated homeland. The muley has the same set of defensive senses as the whitetail and knows how to use them as well as its lowland and eastern cousin, but it relies more on keeping what it considers a safe distance between its precious body and danger than on disappearing entirely like the whitetail. The mule deer is so fast (mulies have been clocked at thirty-five miles per hour)

Mule Deer Buck
(Drawing by Tony M. Sandoval)

that this avoidance tactic is amply successful in protecting him from most predators; however, it often leaves him open for a clean shot with a high-power rifle. Mulies are certainly not dumb but are, as we like to say today, children of a disadvantaged environment.

Mulies, and their several subspecies, range from the Pacific coast to North Dakota and Texas. They are especially well adapted to steep country and can climb like a mountain goat. They add to the whitetail's menu native sages and woody brush which cover much of their territory.

Unlike whitetails, mulies are generally quite migratory, moving long distances between summer and winter ranges. Snow usually triggers their downhill trek in the fall, and they will follow the receding snow line of the mountains back up in the spring.

Elk

The American elk (*Cervus canadensis*), or wapiti, at one time ranged throughout what is now the United States and most of Canada. It is still distributed from coast to coast in the lower forty-eight states but only in pockets. The heaviest concentration of elk today is in the five northern Rocky Mountain states; but other diverse states such as Oklahoma, Texas, Nevada, Michigan, Minnesota, Pennsylvania, New Hampshire, and Virginia have resident populations.

The senses, habits, and habitat requirements of elk are similar to those of mule deer. Major differences are their preference for grazing rather than browsing and their more extensive and specialized territorial demands. Although they have essentially the same defensive tools as mulies, they are inclined to be more cautious and react more vigorously to danger. It is unlikely that an elk, even in the remotest wilderness, will give a hunter the famous "look see" parting shot mulies are famous for.

On the other hand, elk are vulnerable because they tend to be more visible at long distances than deer. They are often found in open parks and meadows grazing during the day. They also tend to let their guard down during the fall rutting-hunting season.

Elk, like mulies, should always be hunted from above because they concentrate their senses on the assumption that dangers come from below.

Also, elk hunters need more of everything than deer hunters, even in the backcountry. In the West horses are the most common way of going after elk not just to get the hunter into the mountain home of the elk but primarily to lug the 600 to 1,000 pounds of meat out of the hills.

Elk rifles should be more powerful than deer hunting rifles, although a well-placed shot with a moderate deer caliber will kill. Most elk hunters prefer heavier doses such as the .300 Magnums, 7 mm Remington Magnum, or even .338 or .375 Magnums. The reason for the heavy artillery is to enable the rifle to drive a heavier bullet over long distances.

Bull Elk
(Drawing by Tony M. Sandoval)

Moose

A century and a quarter ago Henry David Thoreau wrote that the moose "embodied the spirit of the Maine woods." When most people think about moose they think of the wet, heavy veldt of the Maine lakes country. However, economic and hunting pressures have been so intense in Maine that the moose and its remaining habitat has come under strict protection by the state.

The moose used to be abundant through most of the upper tier of states but, although it still exists in most of them, it is a protected refugee in all but a few. Only Minnesota, Montana, Idaho, Utah, and Wyoming continue to have moose seasons in the lower forty-eight states. Alaska and all Canadian provinces have healthy moose populations and continue to allow hunting.

There are several distinct subspecies scattered throughout the range from the giant Alaskan variety, which can weigh nearly a ton, to the half-ton Rocky Mountain variety. Each group has fairly distinct habits and needs; some prefer the timbered flat-lands of the East, while the Rocky Mountain subspecies loves the mountains.

The same preparations and heavier ammunition necessary for elk are needed for moose hunting. Moose are bigger and heavier than elk; so some elaborate funeral arrangements are called for. Many hunters don't think moose are as difficult to kill as the smaller elk, but they are large enough to require a considerable amount of power to kill cleanly.

HUNTING METHODS

Hunting any of these big game animals is merely a matter of acknowledging their strong suits and avoiding them by taking advantage of their defensive behavior traits. All game animals like to travel with the wind in their face. During the day, when you will be hunting them, they will probably be resting as high as they can get to allow the rising thermals to bring signals of danger from below.

The backcountry hunter can either try to bivouac above his game and work down into their beds in the morning or work uphill at daybreak in wide, traversing sweeps which will confuse them by giving only partial danger signals from different directions.

I live on the Flathead Indian Reservation in western Montana. Indians of the Salish and Kootenai tribes here can hunt year around, and many of them do in order to keep fresh meat on the table. A friend of mine, a widely celebrated hunter, has a trick which he uses almost weekly to pin down bedded animals. He starts out with a straight traverse of a hill, watching for a morning trail going uphill. When he finds one, he knows the animal was feeding below him that night and has taken refuge above for a safe snooze.

Starting at the trail, he carefully quarters away from the trail and up about 200 yards, then comes back, crosses the trail, and quarters up in the other direction about 200 yards. He keeps repeating this process, zigzagging across the animal's trail, intersecting it about every 200 linear yards, until he loses it. At that point he carefully works back and forth on a longer arc to make sure the animal did not detour elsewhere, and then he knows his quarry is probably bedded below him.

He picks the downwind side of where he thinks the animal should be and begins working downhill carefully, walking irregularly, knowing the animal has his defenses concentrated downhill but can easily detect an unusual sound behind him. My friend, who is ghostlike in the timber, says he not only normally finds the animal where he expected it but often has to spook it out of bed to get a shot. "It is just a matter of simple geometry and being careful and quiet," he tells me.

Solo Hunting Tactic

This procedure is especially effective in hills or mountains. Stalker cuts a fresh trail going uphill, then zigzags across it at 200-yard intervals until he loses it. He then either waits for the animal to come to him or works carefully back along the route of the trail. (Drawing by Tony M. Sandoval)

Flat-country whitetails will often bed in deep swamp or bush with their nose pointed in the direction of prevailing breezes. Crafty flat-country hunters have a trick called paralleling which can fool even the cagiest bucks. A pair of hunters start by cutting a fresh morning trail. Then they split up on either side of it. One works about 100 feet off on the downwind side; the other moves about 100 to 200 yards (depending on the density of the cover) on the upwind side. They move stealthily through the cover, hoping that the downwind hunter will either get a shot at the animal out of its bed or will spook it into the hunter on the upwind side. If the hunters can clock a pace so they don't get too far behind or ahead of one another, it is a deadly team tactic on all game animals.

Stand hunting—finding a likely place such as a well-used trail, trail junction, or waterhole and quietly sitting downwind of it—is a common and often successful ploy in the early morning and late evening. Western hunters of mule deer and elk have a variation of this called ridge-sitting.

A good ridge is high above two draws animals are known to use with a good field of view for both. Thermals normally come straight up or straight down; so the hunter's scent is probably not going to reach animals in the draws. Ridge-sitting is a waiting game, and I know backcountry hunters who set up a two- or three-day bivouac on the inside of a ridge summit (to protect them from prevailing winds at night) and wait until the right animal comes along. One friend has been doing this for the past eight years and always comes back with meat. It isn't the most exciting form of hunting, but he says he gets a lot of reading done while he is waiting and has even developed a way of perusing the book with one eye and watching points in draws with the other.

Among the many advantages of light-pack nomad hunting is the fact that you do not have to get back to camp for dinner or sleep. You are free to follow trails as far as they will take you without having to worry about leaving yourself enough time to return because there is nothing to return to; you have everything you need for a night or so on your back.

A couple of years ago some friends and I had backpacked about five miles into the eastern extremity of the Cabinet Mountains in western Montana. We hunted there for a day, seeing several animals but not well enough for shots. That night I packed a light

Parallel Stalk

This is a good way for a pair of hunters to work out an animal in any terrain. Hunter on the downwind side of the tracks tries to stay at least 100 feet off the trail while his partner, on the upwind side, skirts the spoor at 100 to 200 yards. (Drawing by Tony M. Sandoval) bag and fanny pack with the necessities of an overnight trek. The bag and fanny pack weighed only twenty pounds, bulging with such bare necessities as a nylon tarp, bivouac sack, poncho, light stove, trail food, one freeze-dried meal, cup, compass, map, sleeping bag, ensolite pad, rope, emergency kit, and an extra pair of socks.

My knife and cartridges were on my belt and rifle on my back when I told my chums in the morning that I was going on a pursuit of game and wouldn't be back to camp for a day or possibly two.

Dawn had not fully broken when I crossed the trail of what appeared to be a large muley buck heading up a draw for a bed. I started out using the zigzag dodge on him, working up well into the afternoon and still cutting his trail. By that time I had left fall behind and was well into the thin snow of early winter. I decided that my buck was not just going up for a good day's doze but was escaping the pressures of his winter range and headed back up into the security of his snow-blanketed summer home.

I knew he was not far ahead of me because his tracks were fresh and firm in the melting afternoon snow, and I was relatively sure he hadn't been spooked because he was walking in a meandering, feeding fashion.

I decided to change my tactics because I would never catch up with him if I continued carefully zigzagging his straight course. I tested the breeze and found that although it was blowing mostly uphill, it crossed the draw slightly from left to right. So I shinnied up the right side ridge about 200 feet above the draw and perhaps 200 yards from his route and worked my way carefully. As the sun blinked beyond the gathering hills in the west, I made my way down into the draw and found that he was still ahead of me. I decided to stick with him, hoping the day's exertions would have tired him enough to bed down for the night. I set up a simple evening camp beside a tiny rill in the draw.

I didn't dare start the stove because I hoped he was just a wee ways upwind of me so I settled for cold trail food and water for dinner. Since the sky was bright and clear, I didn't bother with the shelter (which would get me off to an earlier start in the morning) and just crawled into my bivouac sack-protected sleeping bag.

I awoke face up to the first glimmering of light, munched on some more trail food as I packed my kit, and headed off into the dawn.

The ridges on both sides were playing out as I neared the summit of the group of hills, and I decided to go back to zigzagging behind him. I cut one zag about 300 yards above my camp and found his trail, but on the next zig another 200 or 300 yards up it was gone.

There were two possibilities: (1) my deer was still bedded innocently someplace within the first 200 or 300 yards downhill of me, or (2) he had smelled enough of me during the night and headed off laterally in one direction or another. If the first possibility were true, I had, in turn, two alternative courses of action: (1) stop in my tracks and wait for him to come to me, or (2) with the uphill thermal in my face, move carefully down to him and try to catch him in bed.

However, if the second possibility were the case, the first option would be a waste of time and the second alternative would give me the bad news quickly. I decided the risk of spooking the deer was better than sitting around all day picking my nose.

I had taken about one step in the implementation of option two when I heard a snort about thirty yards in front of me. I froze into an emergency improvisation of option one posture, hardly daring to put option two's first foot down. It was a nose-to-ear standoff for what, as they say, seemed like a lifetime. The buck finally moved around a clump of rocks and it was all over but the shooting.

Getting above the quarry or approaching it from an angle beyond the range of its senses and having the ability to remain there overnight if necessary are often the keys to successful backcountry hunting. Conditioning yourself to the austerity of a light pack camp is the trick to achieving this mobility.

PLACING OF THE SHOT

Meat is the main reason to go big game hunting in the first place and is the only thing of material value you will come home with. It has considerable value, not only as food for you, your family, or friends but also as the material trade-off for taking the life of an animal. Taking good care of game meat not only assures that it will taste better but is also a binding moral commitment that goes with hunting.

Good meat care starts with the placing of the shot. A quick, clean kill will prevent adrenalin from musking the meat of a wounded or badly frightened animal. Know the vital spots and pick the one that presents the best opportunity at the moment.

The surest kill shot is the heart and lung cavity just behind the joint of the forelegs on a broadside shot or just left of center on a frontal target. A heart shot will kill the animal within seconds. An exploding bullet in the lungs will take a little longer, but only minutes at the most.

TRACKING WOUNDED ANIMALS

Remain stark still after what you feel was a killing shot. If it was a heart shot, the animal will probably stagger and fall almost immediately. A lung-shot animal may not show any immediate signs of being hit and bound away without much melodrama. Wait until after it has either fallen or disappeared; then move carefully up to the spot where it was hit. If it was a lung shot, you will probably find frothy blood and bits of hair. Sit down; give the animal a few minutes to suppress its alarm and lie down. It will be weak and when it lies down, it will begin to stiffen. However, if the animal knows it is being pursued, it can travel far and fast on any little bit of oxygen it can still pump through its blood.

After a few minutes, begin carefully following the animal, watching for blood spoor. If you have given it enough time, it is probably close by, either lying dead or too weak and stiff to get up by the time you get to it.

Deer are not dangerous animals but they don't give up easily and the sharp antlers or hooves of a downed deer can do a lot of damage quickly. Approach them carefully with your weapon ready. If they are still alive, they are undoubtedly suffering; so finish them off quickly.

Heart and lung shots normally bleed well enough to eliminate the need for deliberately draining the carcass, but I usually cut through the animal's jugular as soon as I am sure it is dead. I then lay it belly down with its head downhill while I get ready to field dress.

FIELD DRESSING

Field dresing is like total surgery in that you remove virtually all body organs and attempt to be as clean as possible in doing it. The procedure keeps unwanted visceral juices from tainting the meat.

Many hunters carry two knives for field dressing: a small pocketknife to remove the musk glands or tarsals on the inside of the knees on the hind legs, and a hunting knife for evisceration. They say the musky odor from the glands is almost impossible to wipe off a knife and will flavor the meat if that knife is used on the body cavity. I feel that hands are no less tainted than the knife during the musk gland operation and therefore clean both of them as well as the knife carefully on wet grass, leaves, or anything else handy before proceeding with the same knife.

Cleaning starts at the bottom and works toward the top. Turn the animal on its back with its head downhill. Begin by puncturing the skin around the anus and working the blade around the fatty tissue with your finger protecting the point. Work the blade in far enough so you can feel the outside of the rectum. Then cut up around both sides of the genitals (unless state law requires genitals be left in place) and up along the belly to the diaphragm, protecting the point of the blade with your finger. With the cavity open, spread the rear legs and hack or saw through the bottom of the pelvic bone until it breaks through and the legs fall apart.

Allow the viscera to fall forward toward the head. If the rectum does not come out of its own accord, you may have to do some more surgery; but be careful not to puncture the gut.

Find the heart, tongue, liver, and kidney and put them aside in a safe, clean place, preferably a plastic bag. Roll the animal on its side and allow the guts to spill out. Reach into the neck cavity; pull the windpipe down as far as you can and sever it with your knife. Now the animal is cleaned and you can relax for a minute.

MINIMIZING MEAT SPOILAGE

Killing a game animal is always a mixture of pitched excitement and remorse. It is sometimes hard to think clearly and in sequence afterwards, but killing is only the first step of bringing home the meat; and the quality of the table fare depends on everything being done properly and in sequence.

If you did shoot for the heart-lung cavity, you have spoiled some meat with the bullet. This usually consists of only a few ounces; so there is nothing to get excited about. But blood immediately saturates the ragged-edged tissue around the wounds and will continue to soak into adjacent meat if you don't cleanly cut out the blood-soaked wounds.

One way to avoid damaging meat is shooting for the spine at the base of the skull. Unquestionably this is the fastest and cleanest way to kill, but a bullet that hits just slightly off target may leave a fatally injured deer which can run for hours or even days before dropping.

One of the longest and hottest controversies in big game hunting is the question of when a carcass should be skinned. I know hunters who wouldn't dream of leaving the skin on a downed animal for more than fifteen minutes. They say the flesh, tallow, and fatty tissue between the skin and meat begins affecting the flavor as soon as the blood ceases to circulate. They also feel that the blood saturation of wound areas and the decomposition of the meat is accelerated by the skin. They also note the sooner the carcass is skinned, the sooner it can begin to cool.

On the other hand, at least as many other experienced hunters feel the skin helps protect the meat from dirt, bruising, and abrasion while it is being jostled around in the woods or during transit. They feel the animal's own skin is not as likely to affect the quality of the meat as much as dirt or forest duff.

Some feel the animal should be skinned before it is loaded on a car, when a porous gauze bag can be used to protect it. Others feel you might as well wait until you get the animal home where the skin can protect it until it is ready to cure.

I agree with both extremes. I think it is best to get the skin off the animal as soon as you can without exposing it to dirt or bruising. In the backcountry this means the animal should probably remain fully clothed until you reach the car. Hauling meat out of the backcountry is usually a matter of either dragging or quartering and packing. In either case the possibilities of damage or soiling are too great to leave the meat naked.

HAULING OUT THE CARCASS

Dragging is the easiest way of getting a small animal out if you are on your own. The best way to prepare for a drag is to design the animal as much like a sled as you can. In dragging an animal behind you, tie the front legs up over the head, providing an even center of gravity for pulling and preventing unnecessary friction from the hide by pulling with the natural nap of the hair. Cut off the rear legs below the knees.

Dragging is a snap in the snow, where hair fibers act like sled runners; in dry, brushy conditions or when there are hills or ridges to be surmounted, the hair can become worn pretty fast.

In hauling, where the animal goes down ahead of you, the rope should be attached to the other end. This allows the lay of the hair to remain flat on the animal and insulate the meat from bruises and scrapes on the way down.

Larger animals, such as big deer or elk, should be quartered. Unless you have a compelling need for the hide, it is best to leave it on the quarters to protect the meat from injury and detritus. Smaller quarters of deer, weighing up to about forty pounds, can be stuffed into a soft pack or lashed to your back with a rope harness.

Meat hauling is the one place in the backcountry where a frame pack shines. A strong person can easily carry a 100-pound quarter of elk downhill if the weight is carefully distributed over a frame. You will have to make at least five trips if you are carrying out a quartered animal, one for each quarter and the head plus possibly another for the contents of your pack.

Each load should be carefully planned and balanced; so start by removing excess baggage—all four legs below the knee and the neck above the shoulder. Cut the spine in half about two or three ribs up and split the two sides of the carcass by running your knife between the two ribs on each side. Most elk hunters carry either a hand axe or a large belt saw for splitting the spine lengthwise, but deer can be halved with a small saw or sharp knife.

Put aside the first load and hang the other quarters and loads from a convenient branch which will suspend them at about arm's length. Keep them away from tree trunks where crawling critters can make themselves comfortable while dining at your expense, and try to cover the quarters with a poncho, jacket, or even a shirt to make it a little harder for flying freeloaders.

With map and compass work out the best possible route for the first trip back and note landmarks on the way. Use the same route for succeeding trips. And don't forget to tie some color over an exposed load. Looking like game is not healthy during hunting season.

If you have a chum handy, it makes things a lot simpler. The classic pole carry is easy going for two people. Lob off the legs below the knees and lash the nubs around a stout twelve- or sixteen-foot pole. Pad the pole from your shoulder with a hat or jacket and away you go. With elk or extremely large deer, you can divide a pole carry into two trips by taking a half each time. Again be sure to put some color over your load, and it doesn't hurt to add a joyous aria from *Aida* as you go.

There are people who still fireman-carry deer out, but it seems to me that a deer carcass bobbing along makes too believable a target to take the chance.

COOKING THE HEART AND LIVER

Meanwhile back around the campfire the liver was sizzling in an iron fry pan garnished with onions and fresh mushrooms, with delicate pieces of heart floating around in the gravy . . .

There is little doubt that the first bite of freshly killed game is the greatest reward in big game hunting. Hunting itself is too hard to really be called fun and killing is an ambivalent mixed blessing, but the first mouthful of the first cut is sheer euphoria— a realization of purpose that amply justifies all the sweat and time that has gone into the hunt.

But we are in the backcountry, hunting off our backs, and that precludes the classic iron skillet. The fresh onions and mushrooms and the slab bacon to flavor the meat are a lot of trouble to pack. There are several lightweight aluminum and aluminum-teflon fry pans which can be hauled into the backcountry, and there are sometimes wild shaggy mane mushrooms and umbrella onions around the backcountry at hunting season. But in all probability there will have to be some substitution of method or compromise of ingredients for the victory feast.

The liver and heart dinner (to which you can add the tongue and kidney) is important enough to justify some trouble in preparing for it, even at the risk of prejudicing fate. Health food stores sell dehydrated mushrooms, and dehydrated diced onions are available in bottles in any grocery store. A small sack of each tucked away in your food bag may not be considered impudent by the fates and will go a long way in making the meal memorable. You will also need a pad of butter secreted into your grub and a lightweight fry pan.

With your deer curing under a tree, there is no reason you can't build a celebration cooking fire unless other members of the party are still meatless. The fire need not and should not be a victory blaze but just a humble, happy warm crackle with enough burning wood to supply a nest of hot coals. The liver and heart will be more tender if they are allowed to cook patiently over a steady medium heat. The fluctuating heat of direct fire tends to toughen the meat and could easily scorch it through a thin aluminum pan.

The meat will cook faster and will retain more flavor if the pan is covered. Mix everything occasionally to give all the ingredients their time on the bottom of the pan.

During the past few years I have not bothered with a frying pan on my backcountry hunts. I feel the bulk and noise potential of a skillet is not justified by its value at the end-of-the-hunt-dinner (although I certainly don't object if somebody else in the party is willing to go to the trouble of carrying one). Rather, I have experimented with methods of roasting the heart and liver over open coals, barbarian style. My first few attempts were not raving successes. I started by slicing the liver and heart as though for frying and broiling them on a willow grill over even-burning coals. I found they were tasty but tended to be tough, and the mechanical problems of willow grills (they tend to come apart or burn at awkward moments) usually resulted in singeing or overcooking.

With time and age comes wisdom and eventually I was able to conceive of cooking the liver and heart unsliced; with that inspiration came the notion of spitting them whole as a roast well above the coals. After cooking slowly and gently with rather constant turning, I slice them *à la baron* of beef and serve. The slices are so tender they almost fall apart and most of the flavor is retained inside the firm shell.

CURING THE CARCASS

The rest of the carcass will improve with age. It is an almost irresistible temptation to cut a strip of sirloin off the back, especially if you and the animal are around camp for a few days, but it isn't a good idea because the area around the cut will tend to absorb blood and go bad before it has time to properly cure.

How long should a carcass cure before it is processed? That is a matter of how you intend to process it, where it is hung, how warm the weather is, and whom you talk to. I know people who begin preparation as soon as the carcass is cool to the touch. I know others who wait until the fungus is so thick you can scrape it off with a knife. I personally like to wait until a soft, green fungus starts to form, which in cool, late fall Montana is usually a week to two weeks. I hang the carcass in a shed on the north side of my cabin where temperatures remain fairly constant through Indian summer days and frosty nights.

I like to wrap and freeze cuts off the rear half and make either jerky or sausage from the lesser cuts of the rear and the entire front. I usually cure everything so that the steaks and roast along the back and butt will be tender. When it comes time, I wash the entire carcass down with a sponge and vinegar to remove all the fungus, bone the better cuts for freezer packaging, and strip the rest for the sausage maker or slice it for the smoker.

BUTCHERING

Home meat cutting is not particularly difficult but a beginner should have somebody around who knows meat. The most critical cuts are the steaks from the back, loins, and rump. Considering their value on the plate, the amateur butcher should treat them as carefully as a surgeon does an open heart. The steaks all have a way of identifying themselves by the grain of the meat and if you pay attention to this natural definition, you can't go wrong.

I am inordinately fond of hard venison salami; so I don't consider the boning and bagging of the less than prime cuts any kind of sacrifice. However, if you are extremely partial to roasts, there are several possibilities on the lower hind quarters.

JERKING VENISON

There are many ways of jerking or smoke-drying venison that are satisfactory. Generally the process requires salting and smoke-curing, and any method that will accomplish this will do.

On the Flathead Reservation, and in most other Indian communities in America, jerking venison is not just a way of preserving food, it is a social occasion. When hunters come out of the hills with meat, they gather up their families—which usually means everybody from grandparents to grandchildren and anybody else who can remotely be referred to as kin—and meet behind somebody's house.

The women flake the meat, which means cutting it into strips by following the grain of the flesh with a sharp knife, while the men rustle up a sufficient supply of hardwood. In western Montana that usually means hawthorn, apple, or cottonwood.

The open air smoking rack can be made in two basic ways: (1) a number of bars suspended over the fire pit on forked sticks, or (2) fine meshed wire, such as chicken fencing, stretched over the pit. In either case the drying surface is usually from two to three feet over the pit.

A broad fire is started in the pit and allowed to burn itself into a slow, smoking, smoldering sizzle.

Meanwhile, the strips are reposing in a kettle or pot containing strong brine. They are left to absorb the salt while the fire is simmering down to a cloudy smudge, which usually takes about one hour.

The strips are then either skewered onto the rods or placed on top of the screen, and everybody gathers around while the heat and the smoke from the fire gradually warp the juicy slices into hard, crisp wafers. With a wire screen, the meat has to be turned to cure both sides properly.

When the meat is cured, which takes from one-half to two hours, depending on how much smoke and heat reach the strips, it is removed and replaced with fresh strips.

Everybody eats their fill while the meat is warm, but eventually the supply outstrips the immediate demand and dried strips begin accumulating to cool.

Theoretically, jerky will keep almost indefinitely, the variables being the appetites of those with access to it and the way it is stored. Jerky, and any other smoke-cured food, should be stored in a cool, dry place such as an unheated basement room or a root cellar. If the meat is properly cured, the only way it can spoil is through the action of anaerobic bacteria (bacteria which live in the absence of oxygen). It should be stored in well-ventilated containers such as flour sacks or old pillow cases and suspended off the ground where it will be exposed to air circulation and be out of reach of mice and other crawling vermin. Smoked food should never be stored in air-tight jars or sealed plastic bags.

SALVAGING THE NONEDIBLE PARTS

Everything in nature has value; this, by all means, applies to the nonedible parts of your game animal.

Hides, for instance, can be used for a variety of purposes ranging from tying next summer's supply of backcountry trout or bass flies to making clothing. If you are not the handy kind, the whole hide can be sold (in most states) so that somebody else can use it.

Tanning a hide is one of the great ordeals of humankind; unless you have already done a hide and know what you are getting into, let a professional do it. There are several books on making deer-hide clothing and moccasins, and this can be an enjoyable way of whiling away the winter.

Using a hair-on deerskin or elkskin as a surrogate bearskin rug in front of the hearth may sound charming, but the hair is hollow and brittle and it won't be long before it is all over the room.

One deerskin can supply an amateur flytier with enough hair to tie a lifetime supply of Bassbugs or Rat Face McDougals. The hide doesn't have to be tanned in order to use it. I usually salt down the flesh side and stretch it out on a sheltered outside wall with the hair in. When it dries, I cut off the tail and cut the hide into one-foot squares. I usually end up giving or swapping most of the pieces away to other flytiers because I have a hard time using one of them a year.

It takes a little more imagination to find some use for bones and hooves. Paleolithic hunters needed them for tools, implements, and weapons; but there are few people who would argue that a bone awl, as charming as it is, is more efficient than a steel needle.

I am afraid I haven't gotten beyond the Fido stage of bone disposal and even this has its drawbacks. Deer bones, especially, tend to give dogs an enormous amount of gas. Also, it is often said that deer meat and bones create worm problems with dogs. I have found, however, that if the stripped bones are boiled quickly in a large pot and then stored in a bag, dogs are able to digest them with less negative feedback; and I, at least, haven't noticed an especially pronounced worm problem.

CHAPTER 7

Backcountry
Bird Hunting

Most game birds, like big game mammals, place little value on humankind's great works. Most feel more comfortable when they have as little to do with civilization as possible, and some are so unimpressed with their two-legged neighbors they can't even tolerate an occasional encounter.

There are exceptions to this rule. These are not based on any kinship with man but rather on habitat requirements that compel some species either to live on the fringe of civilization or stop in from time to time en route to someplace else.

The most obvious example of such an exception is the ring-necked pheasant. This import from Asia spends his entire life within earshot of man and his machines because he happens to need what man has to offer. Waterfowl, particularly migrating ducks and geese, are another example of birds that are compelled by habitat requirements to share man's living space.

Most native game birds have managed to survive three hundred fifty years of gradually intensifying human settlement on this continent primarily by staying as far away from the action as they could get. Grouse, turkey, snipe, woodcock, chukar, ptarmigan, and several species of quail have managed to avoid the fate of the passenger pigeon by avoiding that forlorn species' fatal mistakes. Some species of waterfowl such as the teals and wood ducks also go to a great deal of trouble to minimize their exposure to civilization.

The farther away from the beaten path you travel, the more likely you are to find these misanthropic birds. This means the backcountry—the remote streams, ponds, and potholes where the timid dabbling ducks take refuge while mankind is declaring war on their larger cousins down country. The out-of-the-way marshy ground around these backwaters is where you will find most of the migrating snipe and woodcock. The woodland grouse (the ruffed, blue, sharp-tailed, and Franklin) are found throughout much of the dense northern forest; ptarmigan, chukar, and mountain quail find sanctuary among the sparsely vegetated hillsides and mountains above the woods.

GROUSE

The most common and popular of these backcountry-loving upland birds are, of course, the grouse. The ruffed grouse (*Bonasa umbellus*) is practically synonymous with American shooting sports. It has held its own well, better than most of its gallinaceous cousins, against the onslaught of cultivation and concrete, continuing to inhabit a wide bank of northern forests which stretches from the Pacific Northwest to New England and the Appalachians. It survives in relative abundance because, like the whitetail deer, it has intelligence, prodigious fertility and the ability to adapt, if compelled, to a variety of habitats and food sources.

The celebrated cunning of the ruffed grouse that hunters commonly encounter on the fringes of civilization melts into silly innocence the deeper one travels into the woodland backcountry. The wild, low, long flushes of educated birds which seem calculated to give the hunter a heart-stopping fright are transformed into lazy flights into openings or fluttering hops into the nearest tree.

As often as not, the biggest problem the wing shooter faces is getting these backcountry bumpkins to flush for a reasonably sporting shot. In the West, twenty-two rifles are the most common grouse guns, with the sporting trick being cleanly placed head shots. A lot of people, including myself, carry a slingshot during big game season in the West (normally overlapping the upland bird season), which makes it possible to put some poultry on the dinner menu of a big game camp.

Ruffed grouse are happy as long as they are in the woods, although they may have seasonal preferences for the kind of forest. Deciduous trees—such as cottonwood, willow, aspen, or poplar in the West and oak and other hardwoods in the East—are preferred during the early fall; conifers, for obvious reasons, are more desirable after the leaves have fallen.

Grouse, being closely related to barnyard chickens, are about as omnivorous as a bird can be. They have a fine eye for nourishment. Crop analysis usually provides an array of vittles ranging from insects (which are fairly rare) through the normal run of berries, leaves, and shoots to twigs and grasses. I have never seen a grouse crop that wasn't an epicurean mixed bag.

In the West, the ruffed grouse has a larger cousin known as the blue or dusky grouse (*Dendragapus obscurus*). This bird doesn't have the characteristic head ruff of the family and is nearly twice as heavy as his better-known relatives. Blue grouse range a bit further south along the Rockies than the ruffed and are found as far south as New Mexico. Blues are not found at all east of the Continental Divide.

The blue is regarded as a prize because of its size and rarity in well-traveled areas, but it is quite as common as the ruffed in the backcountry wooded hills and along timberlines of mountains. Blues, like backcountry ruffed, tend to be all too generous about presenting easy shots and are usually hunted with a twenty-two or slingshot.

The Franklin, spruce, or fool hen (*Canachites*) inhabits the upper reaches of the ruffed grouse's range and is found in the United States only in Idaho, Montana, upper Wisconsin, the Upper Peninsula of Michigan, and northern New England. It is normally scorned by ruffed grouse purists because of its charming way of making easy targets, but it will flush and there is hardly a tastier bird anywhere.

The sharp-tailed grouse (*Pedioecetes phasianellus*) is a prized member of the tribe that is having difficulty holding on to some of its former range, which stretched in the United States from Washington to the Upper Peninsula of Michigan. It has more or less the same habitat requirements as the ruffed but tends to prefer brushy, flat country.

The sage grouse (*Centrocercus urophasianus*) is the most picturesque of the grouse tribe, some say the best-tasting, and probably the most inaccessible for most people. It inhabits the western prairies from Montana to eastern Washington and Oregon.

The sage is the largest of the grouse, weighing up to seven pounds, and lives on the high prairie mostly on sage and other native prairie plants. It can be found near roads and settlements on the plains but is more abundant in out-of-the-way areas where it does not have to compete with cattle or deal with cultivated lands.

CHUKAR

The chukar, like its relative, the Hungarian or gray partridge, was brought to North America from Europe. Unlike its more civilized cousin, the chukar prefers high, desolate, arid foothills and steppes and is consequently game for the backcountry hunter. Its current range consists of a north-south belt from western Montana to eastern Washington down to southern California to Utah. It is colorful and tasty although quite small (only slightly larger than a bobwhite quail).

Chukars are a covey bird and even the wildest of them are good flushers if you hunt them downhill, the direction they tend to fly.

QUAIL

Of the true quails, only the mountain quail of the west slope can truly be considered a backcountry bird, although both the Gambel's and the California quail can be found in more or less equal density in the uninhabited areas of their range as well as along the fringe of civilization.

The popular eastern bobwhite, like the hungarian partridge and ring-necked pheasant, chooses to take his chances with increased hunting pressures in return for the easier living around rich agricultural areas.

The mountain quail (*Oreortyx picta palmeri*) spends most of the year in the steep arid foothills of the western mountain ranges but retreats to lower country when winter sets in. Like the chukar, it likes to escape from danger by running uphill but will flush in a covey if approached from above.

WOODCOCK

If the ruffed grouse has a challenger as America's favorite upland bird it is probably the woodcock (*Philohela minor*). Good hunters delight in the timberdoodle's erratic, zigzagging flight which separates good shotgunners from the crowd.

The woodcock has a wider distribution than the grouse, being at least a part-time resident of thirty-seven eastern states and four eastern Canadian provinces. Actually, there is no such thing as a resident woodcock because the woodcock is instinctively a migratory wanderluster, moving as much as 2,000 miles between winter ranges and summer nesting areas. Woodcock range generally along the Atlantic coast inland as far as Wisconsin in the summer and along the Gulf states in the winter.

Because it is a vagabond much of the year, the woodcock is only a random visitor to backcountry within its range. It will stop off to prod for a few worms with its sensitive long beak, then move on.

Hunting woodcock is best combined with other pursuits in the backcountry because the bird is an unreliable visitor. Look for it in flat, marshy ground among alders and other thick ground cover—and look quickly.

PTARMIGAN

The only ptarmigan that resides in any number in the United States is the white-tailed (*Lagopus leucurus*). Even at that, the whitetail is a rare bird indeed, inhabiting only the high, rugged mountain terrain of Washington, Montana, Wyoming, and Colorado. Like all the birds of his feather, he has two distinct moults—a summer phase with white underparts and a brownish, grayish top changing in winter to pure white or grayish white.

White-tailed ptarmigan, like most mountain birds, like to flush downhill and about the only way a gunner can get to them is to climb above, which is no mean accomplishment, and hunt down. The whitetail is a highly worthy backcountry game bird.

WILD TURKEY

The Wild Turkey (*Meleagris gallopavo*) is a borderline backcountry bird. This is not to infer that it lacks sporting qualities or flavor, but it generally prefers a habitat which is within range of the day hunter. It is a forest bird but likes milder climates and open woodlands such as grown-over cuts and fire clearings. The wild turkey ranges from southern New England down the Atlantic seaboard to Florida and then west in a band from the Gulf states to the southern central states.

Wild turkeys are not willing fliers and are usually hunted with powerful rim-fire rifles (twenty-two Long rifles or magnums) or with heavy shot in shotguns.

DUCKS AND GEESE

Although most ducks avail themselves of the protection of the wilds, especially during the early morning hunting and nesting seasons, the paucity of water and food in the sticks usually forces their migratory flights into everyday hunting range. A hunter is much more likely to score if he hunts mallards or black ducks in medium to large lakes or slow-moving lowland rivers than if he tries to jump them from the tiny ponds and creeks of the backcountry. Backcountry hunters do better with the dabbling ducks, such as teals and wood ducks, which like the small tree-lined ponds of the deep forest and are generally less gregarious and less tolerant of civilization than other waterfowl. Jump or blind shooting out of backcountry camps can be a productive way of bagging these colorful ducks.

Geese, like ducks, are inclined to be more numerous in accessible lakes and slow rivers than in the backcountry. Extremely heavy pressure can force them to look for sanctuary in the bush, but their demands for food while migrating and the sheer weight of numbers on the northern flights usually compel them to scout farm fields and larger bodies of water.

GOING AFTER THE BIRDS

Getting back after game birds can take many different forms. Preparing for such a hunt is probably closer to equipping for a backcountry fishing expedition than a big game outing. The needs of the quarry, of course, are the principal considerations when deciding on a mode of backcountry travel. Most ducks and geese, for instance, prefer to stop over during their migration on large bodies of water near easily accessible food. The trick is to find out-of-the-way places which offer water birds both accessibility to food and security from other hunters.

Floating

Some states have large, floatable rivers which have remained undeveloped for miles between access points. These wild sections of otherwise tame rivers have a way of obscuring themselves from the humdrum of everyday life. The best way to find them is to carefully examine road maps for areas that do not seem to have access. Then check the area out on more detailed land use maps such as state park or forest service maps or U.S. Geological Survey topographical maps to see if there are any private or public unimproved roads which go into the area. If not, you probably have found a gold mine.

Sections of main navigable rivers that have been passed over by roadmakers and other agents of civilization were usually ignored for good reason. They may flow through steep, mountainous gorges, thick swamps, or some other type of terrain which can affect a backcountry boat trip through it. Topographical maps should be able to tell you why the area has not been developed. If it is a swamp or marsh, symbols on the map will indicate this. If the area is hilly or the river passes through a steep gorge or canyon, the proximity of elevation lines should give you an idea of what to expect.

Neither of these extremes are insurmountable obstacles to a waterfowl hunting float, but you will have to take them into account in your itinerary. You may have to plan on one or more portages around rapids or extra waterproof tarps to protect your camp from surface water in a marshy area.

Your craft should be selected with an eye on the water conditions you may encounter. A canoe is probably the most versatile craft, capable of handling white water or a heavy head wind or maneuvering through channels in a marsh. A rowboat will do, provided it is not aluminum (which is far too noisy) or too heavy to beach or portage if that should be necessary. Rubber rafts or kayaks, which are fine in the summer, should be ruled out in the fall or early winter because of the danger of getting passengers or gear wet.

Include in your plans a pickup at the nearest convenient downstream access point. This will require some idea of how many days you will be on the river and where you will be camping.

All camping gear and extra clothing should be tightly waterproofed in sealed plastic bags. If you should get drenched in chilly fall weather that far away from help, it could be a disaster without dry clothing handy.

Needless to say, stealth and a low profile are essential if you are to surprise ducks on the river. Crouch or sit low beneath the seats, use only one oar to guide the boat from the stern like a rudder, and let the current move you at a natural pace; pretend you are a log.

Tule-lined backwaters and eddies can produce some fine blind shooting over a stool of decoys; so take note of slow-looking bends in the river on your map and keep your eyes peeled for likely spots during the cruise.

Hunting from a Base Camp

There are certainly good theoretical arguments for stalk packing through the woods or hills for upland game birds. Stalk packing is an exremely logical and productive way of hunting big game in the same cover; so why not carry a light pack and hunt while you hike for grouse and other timber birds? The problem is grouse and woodcock move so quickly that most gunners have a hard enough time lining them with just the shirts on their backs, and the addition of a thirty-five-pound pack to move on the swing is too much of a handicap. I know because I have tried it. Besides, I don't see any reason to subject myself to the spartan bivouac existence of nomad stalking when I would actually be more likely to find and shoot birds from a relatively comfortable camp, complete with tent, campfire, and rustic amenities.

The backcountry bird hunting camp can be altogether more casual and relaxed than the militarylike big game bivouac. There is not much point to getting up long before dawn if the birds are still roosting, and a little camp clatter and cheer during the day and around the evening campfire is not going to disturb the birds very much. You can pack in a lot of gear that would be out of the question in a deer hunting camp—skillets, a greater array of pots and pans, double foam mattresses, a tent, and maybe even dog food.

Dogs

Dogs in the backcountry are perhaps more trouble than they are worth unless they are extremely well disciplined. For one thing dogs, especially high-strung hunting dogs, and some wild animals such as bears just don't mix. In the range of the grizzly bear a dog can be a downright disaster, and even black bears can take violent exception to Fido. Dangerous encounters aside, a good hunting dog is going to be distracted by the exciting variety of backbush scents that abound. Chasing deer is an almost irresistible impulse, and porcupines can be tragically interesting to a hunting dog.

In most backcountry areas retrievers are absolutely superfluous. Shooting waterfowl over small ponds and creeks won't present a serious recovery problem, and open forest floors do not make it difficult to find downed upland birds. The exception would be woodcock hunting in thickly vegetated marshes or hunting ducks or grouse in heavy bramble.

There is somewhat more justification for hauling along a flusher or pointer for upland birds. Either can hold scurry-prone backcountry birds and inspire them to flush. In heavy cover these dogs can double as retrievers. However, it is absolutely essential they mind without hesitation and that you always keep in touch with them. A small bell on their collar is handy for keeping tabs and a lead to tether them at night can save a lot of grief later.

Hunting dogs work hard; so either you or your dog is going to have to take an ample supply of dog food. Several backpacking outfitters market dog panniers (double bags which harness over the dog's back), and it is conceivable your dog will tolerate them. My retriever will grudgingly put up with a pair I jury-rigged from two Army gas mask bags, but my setter fancies herself an aristocrat and will have nothing to do with menial labor. If I take her along, that understanding is in the contract.

I let the area determine whether or not I take my setter. If I am going to be hunting open timber or brushy mountainsides I leave her at home. Brushy creek bottoms, marshy areas, or thick timber are more than I can handle by myself; so she gets a ticket. If I do bring the setter, I also bring the retriever to haul the food and to keep her chum in line. Sometimes I wonder who owns whom and which of us is boss.

The trail to and from a backcountry camp can be hunted. If you flush birds along the way, mark their flight, stash your packs where you know you can easily find them (this is not as simple as it sounds, especially if you wander far after the birds), and work them down with your gun. If you run into an unusual number of birds before you get to the place where you had planned to camp, you might reconsider and set up camp where you know them to be. You may have caught them moving down from summer to winter feeding areas and if you go much higher, you could find yourself bereft of birds. This is especially true of mountain quail, Franklin and blue grouse, and ptarmigan.

Waterfowl hunting campsites should be predicated on the attractiveness of the area to native and migratory flights. A small marshy creek with numerous beaver ponds is ideal. Beaver works seldom show on topographical maps because they are geologically ephemeral. But if you can find a creek in a backcountry area which passes through marshy areas (identified on the map by blue hummock signs or extremely mild gradation), you are probably going to encounter ducks.

FOWLING GUNS

The requirements of a backcountry fowling gun are about the same as we discussed in a pack rifle for big game. It should be reliable, sufficiently powerful to do the job, light, short, compact, and handy. To me this means a double-barrel gun with twenty-four- to twenty-six-inch tubes weighing between five and six pounds and bored in either sixteen- or twenty-gauge. My own backcountry fowler is an ancient French St. Etienne side-by-side sixteen which weighs just under five pounds and has a retractable sling spring-loaded into the buttstock. It is choked full and modified, which is tight enough to give its twenty-five-inch barrels enough poop to kill a teal at thirty-five yards, yet is handy and quick enough to follow a dashing woodcock through the brambles. The gun hasn't been made since the 1930s and is hard to find today, but there are several others both old and new that will do as backcountry fowlers.

There are numerous over-and-under guns in twenty-gauge three-inch Magnum made today which are light, handy, and reliable. They range in price from about $300 to well into the thousands. Recently made Spanish, Italian, and Japanese over-and-unders can be bought secondhand for about two-thirds of their new value, or about a minimum of $200.

There are also an appreciable number of Spanish side-by-side twenties, most with 2¾-inch chambers, floating around both new and used. They normally don't fetch as much as over-and-unders, currently around $200 new and as little as $100 secondhand. Some of them are remarkably fine weapons. Of course some of them aren't, and you should check them out carefully before putting all your faith in them for the long backcountry haul. As an added bonus many European guns have sling swivels in the buttstock and brazed into the barrels above the fore end.

Single-barrel shotguns are light, twice as reliable, and less expensive but require twice the confidence, not to mention competence, to trust in only one shot.

Most mechanical shotguns, pumps and automatics, are too heavy as well as subject to malfunction. There are exceptions: the trim little Ithaca Model 37 pump, which has a good reputation for performance and weighs under six pounds in twenty-gauge, and

Lightweight Backcountry Shotgun

This is a sixteen-gauge five-pound double made a long time ago by St. Etienne in France. However, there are any number of light guns available new or second-hand.

the recently discontinued Browning Double Automatic, which could handle two shots about as honestly as any double made and was remarkably light.

Most shotguns are not fitted with swivels; so a gun intended primarily for backcountry use should either be fitted with a pair or some other kind of sling arrangement should be provided. There are currently on the market a few slings designed for shotguns which use friction-fitting loops around the stock and the barrels. They do not require any drilling or brazing and will not impair the value of your gun.

No matter how you arrange it, you should have a sling on your shotgun for the same reasons you need a sling on a pack rifle. You absolutely need both hands for backcountry trail blazing.

CLOTHING

You may need special, waterproof footgear for backcountry fowling. Something as extreme as hip boots is probably not necessary, but water-resistant or waterproof high hunting boots may be well worth their extra weight. All rubber waterproof packs will give you about as much draw as you need in marshy ground but may trap as much moisture in the form of perspiration from your feet during the hike as other boots would ship during a wet hunt. On the other hand, a rubber-bottom, oil-tanned leather-top boot such as the L. L. Bean Maine boot or the Sorel will allow hiking sweat to escape while protecting your feet during mushy stands or shallow wading.

Otherwise clothing should be ample to meet the weather conditions and bright enough to be seen by big game hunters in the area (in many states upland bird and waterfowl seasons coincide with big game hunting seasons).

THE NEED TO AVOID OVERKILL

If you are careful about choosing an area, backcountry fowling can be more productive than hunting down below. Occasionally, the hunting in the backcountry is phenomenal with birds charging from all directions. This normally happens during migration periods when birds of a feather start looking for greener pastures below, or with ruffed grouse, during the mysterious fall crazies when they get together and seem to deliberately fling their souls on the world for no apparent reason.

When you encounter conditions like this in the backcountry, it is tempting to fire away until your barrels melt or you run out of ammunition. After all, you worked hard to get there and one doesn't get a chance to make up for all the dog days very often.

Such a reaction resembles the way weasels behave. Members of that tribe are about the only creatures besides humans which behave in terms of overkill. Otters and mink are infamous for their rapacity in trout or salmon rivers, where they will begin killing for food and then lose control and kill everything they can catch just for the fun of it. A skunk or a weasel will do the same thing in a chicken house: break in for a little snack and before he is done the roost is red with blood. Weasels don't seem to be able to stop killing and wasting energy when their needs have been met.

But they are animals and slaves to their nature. What about people, "sportsmen" who will get blood in their eye when the opportunity avails itself even though they know they can't use all the harvest of their carnage and that they are breaking laws, legal and moral? Are they following the nature of their species or are they aberrant specimens with rotten chromosomes?

I think it is frightfully easy to make an argument for the former case. If sportsmen are not supposed to make pigs of themselves in the wilds, why is it all right for civilized nations to develop enough nuclear overkill to obliterate the biosphere forty times over? After all, enough power to wipe out anything once should be enough for any normally functioning organism. We humans do, it seems, have an unhealthy tendency to overdo things.

While I am at it, I might note that human wantonness has caused the premature obliteration of several species of animals—some in the name of economics and others, like the passenger pigeon, just for the bloody fun of it.

The argument doesn't stop there. Societies, like people, tend to indulge in excess whenever they get the chance. The United States today uses ten times as much water per capita as any other nation in the world and we continue to increase our consumption of that finite commodity as well as most other resources every year in spite of the damage it is doing to us and our land.

I am happy to say that neither I nor any of the people I tromp the backcountry with ever exceed game limits. In fact I don't think I have ever killed anywhere near the legal fish bag and I have established an absolute two bird limit for myself. However, I am not so proud to say that every time I get a chance to kill a third bird, a bird I would probably have to give away, or stuff one more good-sized trout into my bag, the blood swells to my head and I know that I am not so righteous after all. I have to remind myself that killing to eat may be a biological imperative but killing more than you need is a crime against nature. Every time I encounter an overkill situation I have to carefully weigh reason against lust. I don't think I am a freak either. I think most conscientious hunters and fishermen are in a constant struggle between nature and conscience. Conservation is a matter of thought, not reflex, with human beings.

At any rate, the immediate nutritional needs of backcountry fowlers are relatively limited. One bird per day per person is about all that can be consumed. It is true that birds can be stored in cool fall weather for taking back to the folks at home, but there are legal, ethical, and logistical problems.

Most states have a rather tight possession limit, normally about twice the daily bag limit. It would be both embarrassing and expensive to encounter a warden when you return to the car with several days' legal limits in your bag.

On the other hand the ethical question revolves around the propriety of exploiting the backcountry, even in what may seem small and insignificant ways. The reason there are more birds, game, and fish in the backcountry is because the land has escaped exploitation in the past. This is normally a matter of historical and geological accident, but it is a windfall to sportsmen. Responsibility goes along with this bounty. It has to be used in a temperate manner so the interest on the principal can be reinvested to assure the fortune remains intact.

HOW TO EVISCERATE A BIRD

All wild fowl, particularly ducks, should be field cleaned as soon as they are retrieved. It isn't a very big job and it assures that the meat is untainted and will keep through a relatively warm fall day.

The easiest and least messy way of eviscerating a bird is to use a gut hook. Gut hook blades are currently available on several bird knives, or you can use an old button hook or large aluminum crocheting needle. Any fine metal rod at least four inches long with a one-quarter-inch-gap smooth surface hook at the end will do. Insert the rod hook first into the bird's cloaca (vent), twist to catch the intestine around the hook, and retrieve both ends of the loop of intestines. Carefully draw the intestine out until both ends of the loop offer firm resistance. Break them off and the bird is effectively field dressed.

Another and perhaps better, although messier, method is to make a small cut at the anus and probe out all the intestines and organs with your finger. If you can, wash the cavity out to remove blood or tripe that may have escaped a punctured intestine. Cleaned and washed, a carcass will last two or three days if stored in a cool, shady place.

It is wise to leave the feathers on until you are ready either to eat or freeze-store the birds. The skin will insulate the meat from sunshine and heat and protect it from bacterial spoilage.

SKINNING VS. PLUCKING

Whether you skin or pluck the bird is primarily a matter of preference and time. It is faster to skin but plucking preserves the tasty and nutritious skin on the meat. The skin will also retain body juices during the cooking process and provides a more tender cooked bird. If you are going to pluck the bird, do it as quickly as possible, preferably while the bird is still warm, because the quill ends tend to set in a cooled bird.

Skinning is so easy I usually end up, in spite of good intentions, doing that rather than tediously plucking a camp bird. Tear the skin forward along the belly from the anus to the breast. Pull it out from around one leg, break the leg at the junction of the leg and feather, and cut it off. Do the same to the other leg and pull the skin off the back a ways. Cut the fleshy flange holding the tail and pull all the skin up to the wings. Repeat the leg process on the wings, breaking the wing just above the first primary feathers. Pull the skin, crop and all, up to the head and cut off the gullet.

TASTY WAYS TO COOK FOWL

For me, cooking birds over a campfire is no bother or problem at all. I like them spitted and slowly turned over hardwood coals until they are about equally cooked and smoked. Any other standard cooking method from frying to dutch oven baking will do if you are properly equipped.

Shaggy mane mushrooms (*Coprinus comatus*) happen to coincide with upland bird season throughout most of the northern states. There is nothing shaggy manes go better with than grouse and vice versa. They fry well together. Just cook the grouse in bacon fat or butter until it is minutes from being ready; then add the mushrooms to the pan. I have had some really amazing dutch oven campfire concoctions (cooked by someone else) involving grouse or ducks, shaggy manes, and a few other mysterious ingredients. If you understand the wondrous workings and potentials of dutch oven cookery, the world is your plum.

USES FOR THE NONEDIBLE PARTS

The nonedible parts of most game birds, like those of big game, can be recycled into your backcountry sporting bag. As most fly fishermen know, wood duck flank feathers are literally worth their weight in gold. They are virtually unobtainable on the open market and are essential for winging many traditional American fly patterns. Wing and body feathers from virtually all upland birds and waterfowl are useful for wings and hackles on flies.

The down on ducks and geese also has more than passing value. A friend of mine, an ardent waterfowler, takes a large shopping bag with him whenever he goes hunting and carefully sorts and saves all the useful down. He even goes so far as offering to pluck the birds shot by total strangers and keeps the down for his trouble. During the winter, he and his wife mull around the sewing machine making clothing and outdoor equipment for their family.

CHAPTER 8

Backcountry Hobbies

There is more to the backcountry than just raw protein. It is a community of plants and animals structured by the character of the land into which we travel as tourists.

As tourists we can admire and study a variety of local attractions that will give us a greater appreciation for this strange country.

We can record what we see and do on film. Photography is now well within the budget and competency of just about anyone and, as a backcountry hobby, goes well with other pursuits. Birding, the identification of birds and cataloging of observations, is another way of expanding our knowledge and feeling for the backcountry.

During the temperate months, flowers and plants can add spice to a backcountry outing and can tell you a lot about where you are. Plants and berries can be a delightful primary or supplementary source of backcountry food.

PHOTOGRAPHY

Taking pictures during our travels gives permanence to the trip by giving us a visual record.

Equipment for backpacking photography can run anywhere from simple miniature cameras no larger than a fat cigar to a well-stocked studio, depending on what you can afford to put into your gear and what you expect to get out of it.

Cameras

Most people who are fishing or hunting will want at least a snapshot or two of the things they have done and the places they have seen. For this there is probably nothing better than an inexpensive, tiny 110 cartridge camera available from many drug stores. These cameras range in price from about $10 to $175. The lower end requires a little bit of guesswork and may not have the quality necessary for fine, sharp snaps. Starting with the middle lower bracket, 110's are usually automatic, give you sharp focus and better exposure, and offer better optics.

The top of the 110 line is the Minolta 110 SLR. This camera will do just about anything a sophisticated 35-mm will do but on a smaller negative.

For those snapshooters who want a little more negative to work with, for large blowups or fine printing, there are a number of palm-sized miniature 35-mm rangefinder cameras available from $50 to $400. Cameras in the lower end of the price range have most of the same faults as the cheap 110's, but for about $100 there are several which will do most of the work for you and produce excellent snaps and workable negatives. One of the best cameras in this category is the Rollei 35. It has a good sharp lens and automatic exposure control which can be manually over-ridden. It is sufficiently rugged (I have banged one around for a couple of years), reliable, and remarkably versatile.

Or you can spend about $400 on a Leica CL, the aristocrat of miniature 35's. For your hard-earned money you will get the best name in the business, an interchangeable lens capacity, and a through-the-lens metering system which is an advantage when using lenses of various focal lengths and filters. You also get all the basics found on other cameras and Leica's world-famous crys-

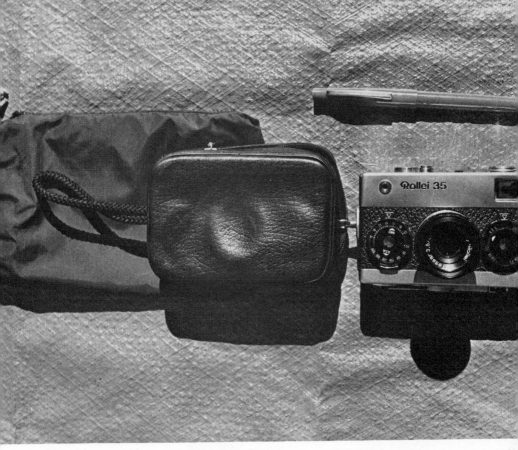

Carry-along Camera

Several firms are making tiny full-frame 35-mm cameras that can do most of the things huskier cameras can do. This one is a Rollei 35 which collapses into a case the size of a cigarette pack. In its waterproof nylon bag it is safe in most any available cranny of your pack.

tal-sharp Leitz lenses. The camera will use either a special series of lenses, a 40-mm normal and a 90-mm short telephoto, or standard Leitz bayonet mount lenses.

The next step up in terms of cost, bulk, and versatility would be any of a number of new, compact full-frame 35-mm single-lens reflex cameras. These cameras offer a full range of lenses from very wide-angle to long telephoto, automatic or manual exposure control, through-the-lens viewing, and focusing precision. All these features are contained in amazingly small, light packages. The Olympus OM-1, for instance, weighs just 1½ pounds with a normal 50-mm lens. Other lenses in the system are light and compact. A backpacking photographer could be equipped with a normal, a wide-angle, and a telephoto lens and extra film with just a 2½-pound package.

I have used an OM for a year and have found it rugged and reliable. The OM-1 is currently available for about $250 with normal lens. Two other firms are now distributing comparably compact 35-mm SLR's. They are the Canon AE-1 and the Asahi Pentax ME. Both of these cameras are slightly more expensive than the OM-1, as is Olympus's sequel, the OM-2.

Lenses

A normal 40- to 50-mm lens or moderately wide-angle lens, 28 to 35 mm, is ample for most backpacking photographic needs. Either will handle scenics and group or individual shots and won't require a tripod or other special (and heavy) equipment in bad light.

The only situation where telephoto lenses, from 100 mm on up, are necessary is photographing wildlife. They permit the photographer to overcome the timidity of wild critters by bringing the animals closer optically, like binoculars. A 100-mm telephoto lens would be the equivalent of two-power binoculars. A 200-mm lens equals a four-power set of binoculars, and so on. On the surface, it would seem that the more powerful the lens the better because you can snap wildlife pictures from a greater distance. However, the formula is not as simple as it may seem.

In the first place, a telephoto lens must be longer and heavier than normal lenses to allow the magnified image to develop in the optics. The more powerful the lens, the bigger, heavier, and clumsier it is. Most 300-mm (six-power) lenses are well over a foot and weigh over two pounds. Even if you don't object to hauling one of these monsters around, you are still going to have problems holding onto it. The longer the lens, the more critical is the focusing, to a point where focus tolerance is measured in inches over a range of hundreds of feet, and the more difficult it is to keep the image from blurring on the negative. With a 40-mm lens (short normal) a reasonably steady person can shoot a clear, unblurred photograph with a hand-held camera at ¹/₃₀ second. Using a 300-mm lens, a professional with years of experience would have

Lightweight Photo System

Although single-lens reflex 35-mm photo systems have undergone drastic minia-turization, they are still too heavy and bulky to carry casually in your pack. This is one of the lightest and most compact SLR systems available—the Olympus OM-1 with 35-mm, 50-mm, and 200-mm lenses—yet it still weighs over two pounds and requires a great deal of pack space. When I am using this much gear, I carry it in a separate bag such as the Maran Carry-On pictured. Other gear in-cludes binoculars, tripod, and extending monopod.

trouble holding the camera steady enough at $1/1000$ second, the fastest speed most cameras provide. Long telephoto lenses, start-ing at about 300 mm, absolutely require a tripod and cable shut-ter release. You can count on an additional two pounds or more and a lot of bulk with this extra gear.

When I do take an SLR into the backcountry, which is seldom and only if photography is the main reason I am going, the longest lens I take is a 200-mm. I can usually hold the 200-mm steady enough at $1/500$ second to get a good negative; sometimes, with the support of a handy tree or rock, I manage a tolerable negative at $1/250$ second.

Camera Supports

There are ways of hedging on the long lens wiggle factor that do not require the additional bulk of a tripod. A professional photographer friend of mine hikes with a bamboo walking stick containing a tripod lug glued into the top. When he needs the support for a long shot in difficult light, he jams the end of the stick into the snow or steadies it against something and screws the camera into the lug. He knows what he is doing and gets away with 200-mm shots at $1/125$ or even $1/60$ second. I have also seen tripod lugs soldered into the top of backpack frames, which is a fine idea, but setting them up is a bit more awkward than most photogenic animals are going to put up with. I have tried a variety of steadying implements from a folding monopod to a trigger-operated pistol grip and found that none of them was really worth the bother. The process of digging the camera out, finding and pitching the steadying aid, connecting the camera, and messing around with camera adjustments usually puts wild creatures to tail.

Instead, I have tried to develop a good eye for natural supports. Sometimes I lie down in a prone position and take my chances with hand-held long-lens shots. If my negatives are not calendar quality, at least I am getting something of interest in them.

Fast Film

Another way of stacking the odds in your favor with mid-range telephoto equipment is to use fast film. I normally shoot Kodak Tri-X black and white film, which has a relatively fast normal speed of 400 ASA. The ASA equation tells you how fast the emulsion on the negative is exposed. The higher the ASA, the quicker the emulsion absorbs the light image and the faster you can set your shutter speed in a given light situation. Tri-X can be safely pushed (that means accelerating the film processing) to 800 ASA, and that is what I usually do to compensate for spartan backpack exposure conditions.

There are also a number of good-quality speedy (up to 500 normal ASA) color films for 35 mm available. Color films are more sensitive to exposure and tonal integrity than black and white, and you have to know what you are doing to push color beyond the recommended speed.

Camera Protection

Most cameras are extremely susceptible to damage by water and rough handling. These are two of the most common elements in the backcountry; so your equipment should be well protected.

There are commercial waterproof and shock-absorbing cases available. Maran Packs of Bigfork, Montana makes custom-fitted camera and lens cases that are water-resistant and practically shockproof. Several firms are making zip-top heavy vinyl waterproof camera bags. Almost as good, however, are your spare wool socks pulled over the camera or lens and sealed in heavy-gauge freezer storage bags with twist tops. I also have a waterproofed nylon bag which fits over the top of my compact camera and has drawstrings on the bottom. This shields the camera against body moisture or light precipitation while I am carrying it around my neck, and can be removed in a jiffy if I am in a hurry to get a picture of a charging grizzly or something equally exciting. If it starts to drizzle, I stash the camera under my waterproof jacket and if it develops into a heavy rain, I put it in the waterproof bag in my pack. So far, I haven't lost a camera to drowning.

If you are reasonably careful, you shouldn't lose too many cameras to concussion either. The sock and judicious packing should protect your camera in the pack. You can keep it from banging into things while it is around your neck by wearing it under clothing or bound under the belly strap of your pack.

Developing an Eye for Composition

Taking good, worthwhile photos is a matter of a good eye, not necessarily good equipment. A friend of mine defines the art of photography as "the only human endeavor where one can create a masterpiece by accident." He is right. Anybody including a monkey can take exhibit-quality pictures because of the relatively limited mechanical processes of the craft. If the shutter and f-stop are correctly set for exposure, the lens is in focus, and the subject happens to be right, your dog stepping on the shutter could accomplish feats of high art.

However, to consistently get satisfactory pictures, you have to develop an eye for composition and a feeling for delicate exposure requirements. Framing a picture of a friend with a nice trout in front of an idyllic mountain lake with the peaks shining in the background isn't going to make his scrapbook much less his wall if you cut the top of his head off, underexpose the brilliant color of the fish, or lose the mountains in a blur. You have to learn what your lens will put into the negative, how to compensate in f-stop exposure for the difference in distance between your chum and the mountain, and how to read your meter and the light to know whether both the fish and the mountain will be properly exposed. These are not the kind of thing you can learn overnight, camera notwithstanding, and you won't get everything you need out of a book. The only way to learn is to take pictures, preferably with someone who knows what he is doing.

There is no practical difference between a technically good picture taken in your back yard and one shot on top of the Garden Wall in Glacier National Park; so practice at home can save a lot of disappointment with your pictures of a once-in-a-lifetime backcountry expedition.

There are several good basic guides available. One of the best is the pocket-sized *Kodak Master Photoguide*, which costs $2 and will tell you at least as much as you need to know about the basic mechanics of photography.

LEARNING ABOUT PLANTS

The wildlife of the backcountry does not end with game and fish. There is a whole dimension of wild, glorious things back there that can please the palate, charm the eye, and tantalize the senses. Plants, from the lowly fungi to the lofty pines, are as much a part of the backcountry experience as the stalk or the cast. The more you know about them, the more you will understand and enjoy all the character of the land.

Plants, like animals, are where they are because they are part of the fabric of the environment. The flowering, budding, popping, and towering flora might have been made for the convenience and enjoyment of backcountry travelers. Much of it is edible, tasty, and wholesome (although some plants are highly toxic), most are dazzlingly beautiful in their season, and some can even help you find out where you are.

Many plants grow only at certain altitudes or in very limited environmental conditions. The red or alpine heather, for instance, grows within a fairly narrow band of mountain terrain. Other plants, such as skunk cabbage and many of the willows, will grow only in swampy or water-saturated soil. Cedar and juniper trees in the West and hemlocks in the East will also tell you there is water nearby. Trees can also reveal how high you are in the mountains. At the edge of the timberline in our western mountains (from 8,000 to 10,000 feet) the only trees which grow vigorously are subalpine fir and Engelmann spruce. Other trees are stunted and distorted. Above timberline only vegetation that can protect itself from the harsh alpine elements survives. These are mostly shrubs that root in the lee of rocks, slopes, or cliffs. Much of this mountain vegetation is, like the backpacker, a stranger visiting a strange land.

Wild Flowers

The summer backcountry is a veritable garden of dazzling color and form. Some hardy flowering plants and shrubs begin blooming as soon as temperatures begin to moderate in the spring, sometimes poking out of snowbanks to get a head start on summer. Others bloom from late summer until they are covered with snow in the fall. This carpet of delight provides a bright, shimmering kaleidoscope of color for the seasonal hiker, a brilliant background for backcountry photos, and an interesting subject for occasional study.

Knowing the wild flowers can add an element of appreciation to their charm. Most states and even areas within states have published guides to local wild flowers. National and state parks and state departments of fish and game, conservation, or natural resources often have wild flower bulletins available. Also, the excellent Peterson Field Guide Series has regional wild flower handbooks which can be purchased at most book stores. Knowing the difference between Saint-John's-wort and a yellow monkey flower not only adds to the fascination of the plant but can also tell you something about the place it grows.

In many states it is illegal to pick orchids because of their rarity and the time it takes to develop a flower. Many other wild flowers have to struggle for roots in a barren environment, and it is unwise to pick them while they are in the process of reproduction. Just admiring them where they are and remembering them or photographing them will prove more satisfying than a wilted souvenir and will assure they will be back again next year.

Edible Wild Plants

Many plants have a practical as well as aesthetic value. Nearly every area of the United States abounds with free trailside lunches for the picking or digging. In season wild berries can furnish most of the trail food for a hard day's hike. Mushrooms and the parts of other plants can add zest and variety to camp meals. Even in the hard winter there are berries, plant roots, and fibers that can help sustain the backcountry traveler in an emergency.

Not all plants are nourishing or even edible and some plants and parts of otherwise edible plants are dangerously poisonous. For instance, most species of camas are at least moderately toxic and some are extremely dangerous. However the Indian camas (*Camassia quamash*) is not only edible, it is extremely nourishing and delicious when the roots are properly roasted.

The common chokecherry (*Prunus melanocarpa*), which is found just about everywhere in the United States, is eminently edible down to the pit, which, along with the leaves, is poisonous.

To put it another way, there is really no such thing as a free lunch; the trailside muncher is going to have to devote some study and effort to identifying plants which can be safely eaten.

There are several excellent guides to edible plants available. Among them is Bradford Angier's *Field Guide to Edible Wild Plants,* available in both a standard and pocket-sized edition.

Plants that are poisonous to eat are not the only leafy perils in the wilds. There are also several members of the sumac family which can cause annoying and dangerous inflammation if touched.

These are poison ivy (*Rhus radicans*) and its relatives poison oak, poison sumac, and squawbush. These plants produce a caustic oil called urushiol which reacts violently with skin on contact. Know them and avoid them like the plague they are.

There are hundreds of species of edible plants common throughout the United States and thousands that are found regionally. Here is a baker's dozen of plants that occur just about everywhere. The list includes mushrooms, berries, and plants to give you a sampling of the culinary variety that abounds in the backcountry.

Cattail

Cattails, members of the Typhaceae family, are familiar to just about everybody with their long, reedlike leaves and hot dog-shaped seed cluster at the top of a thin stalk. They grow abundantly in marshy areas throughout the United States.

The root and the lower base of the leaves are an excellent salad green in the spring and summer. The stalk, when young, is widely regarded as a delicacy boiled while the seed pod, before it turns brown, has a tender, cornlike texture and a fine, delicate taste when boiled and eaten like corn.

Wild Onion or Garlic

Several varieties of the *Allium* tribe are found nearly everywhere in the United States in diverse terrain ranging from low marshy areas to somewhat arid slopes.

The three most common *Allium* plants are the wild onion (*Allium stellatum*), wild leek (*Allium tricoccum*), and wild garlic (*Allium canadense*). All three can be identified by their umbrella-like flower stems which radiate over the top of eight- to twelve-inch thin, round stalks. The onion and garlic have clusters of long, onionlike leaves that stand erect from the bulb. The leek has two broad textured leaves which protrude from the root bulb about halfway up the stalk.

You can usually smell the wild onions before you see them but if you break the stalk, there is no mistaking the eye-watering aroma.

Wild Onion

The bulb, leaves, and stalk are an excellent onion substitute as flavoring for main dishes. If you have the stomach for spicy tidbits, you can munch on them raw as a trail snack.

Salsify

Goatsbeard, oyster, oyster plant, and meadow salsify are the names these plants of the genus *Tragopogon* are known by from coast to coast.

The plant has a long, slender stalk with yellow or purple toothed flowers on the top and a gnarled oysterlike root beneath. Leaves node from the stalk and are moderately long and flat.

Just about all of the plant has food value, starting with the root, which when boiled has a texture similar to and a flavor not unlike oysters. In the spring and early summer the root, leaves, and stalk can be cut up and added to salads. Later in the year, after the plant matures, the greens can be boiled and eaten as a vegetable. The root and greens can be dried or roasted and ground to make a coffeelike beverage.

Salsify is not only nutritious, it is also deemed a cure for indigestion.

Salsify

Wild Mustard

Mustard, a member of the *Cruciferae* family, adds beauty with its small pale yellow flowers to much of the countryside. It can also contribute great flavor to backcountry camp fare.

The plant has broad, oaklike leaves stemming from a long, narrow stalk. Radiating around the stalk are small pod stems which contain seeds and will flower at maturity.

The pods are the source of the mustard seed which is processed into mustard paste of pastrami and hot dog fame. You can make a mustard garnish by grinding the seeds and mixing with water into a paste or you can toss some seeds into a green salad or soup for extra zest.

In the spring and early summer, the greens are tasty either as a salad or boiled as a vegetable.

Primrose

Found in arid ground throughout the United States and Canada, the primrose is celebrated widely for its tasty root.

Wild Mustard

Primrose
Left: *Rosette*. Right: *Stalk with leaves, flowers, and seed capsules.*

The plant has a relatively wide, hairy stalk intersected from root to top by flat, jagged leaves. It has a two-year cycle, growing to maturity with flowers the second year. The roots are best on first-year plants. They are excellent boiled and eaten by themselves or added to other dishes.

Highbush Cranberry

Wild cranberry, a member of the honeysuckle family (Caprifoliaceae), is not only a zesty berry but also an important year-round survival food.

The berry grows on a tall woody bush in heavy clusters among broad, three-pronged leaves.

The wild berry has a snappier flavor than its domesticated Thanksgiving Day cousin and provides both nutrition and essential Vitamin C. During the temperate months, the berries are juicy and tender. They can either be eaten raw right off the bush or cooked to make syrup or a jam. In the winter, the berries remain on the tall bushes as shriveled little kernels in clusters. The bushes, which sometimes grow eight feet tall, often protrude from deep snow and offer these tangy-sweet berries to the winter traveler.

Highbush Cranberry
Top: *Leaves and fruit.* Bottom: *Blossoms.*

Wild Raspberry

The wild raspberry bush with its rough sawed leaf is familiar to most people who spend any time outdoors. The bushes grow along hedgerows and roads and in open fields across the northern part of the United States and grace the backcountry within this range as well.

Nobody has to be told what to do with raspberries, and they are as nutritious as they are tasty. The leaves of the bush also make an excellent and hearty tea, either dried and crushed or right off the bush.

Serviceberry

One of the most common wild berries throughout the United States and Canada, with species of the genus *Amelanchier* growing as far south as Mexico, is the serviceberry.

Serviceberries grow on bushy trees which sometimes reach fifteen or twenty feet. They like their ground wet and are often found along the fringes of ponds or lakes or along creeks.

The buckshot-sized berries with green leafy tufts protruding from the ends virtually cover a tree at maturity. Although quite

Serviceberry
Left: *With fruit.* Right: *With flowers.*

wholesome, the serviceberry has a seedy, waxy texture which is not quite as attractive as other wild berries, but its seasonal abundance and availability makes it an important backcountry food.

Huckleberry

The huckleberry (*Vaccinium*) and the wild strawberry (*Fragaria*) are probably the two choicest wildwood snacks.

The huckleberry reaches one-quarter to one-half inch in diameter, depending on the area and the growing conditions. The bush, with its lustrous, sharply pointed leaves, ranges in size from a ground bush to a respectably large hedge. Huckleberry bushes often grow in thick colonies, and hikers in July and August can spend a delightful hour or so plucking berries and gobbling them for lunch.

The huckleberry is also a favorite of black and grizzly bears, and territorial conflict between pickers and bruins is fairly common.

If you haven't tasted huckleberries, there is no way of describing their sweet-tart bite, and if you have, there is no need to.

Shaggy Mane Mushrooms

The shaggy mane and its *Coprinus* relative the inky cap are probably the two most common and abundant edible wild mushrooms. They, like most other mushrooms, are found in well-watered soil near ponds and streams.

Both are distinctive and can be easily identified by the black, inky substance that begins forming around the lower gills and eventually consumes the cap. The shaggy mane can also be spotted by the upward curling flakes on the cap which give it its name.

These mushrooms grow in colonies, and only specimens which have not started to ink should be selected for eating. They should be cooked as quickly as possible because deterioration begins almost immediately. Fried, they are quite delicious by themselves or as added body to other dishes. In the western mountains, inkies emerge in the spring with shaggies following in the fall.

Puffballs

The giant puffball (*Calvatia gigantea*) appears suddenly overnight like an ivory-white watermelon. It has a wide range and grows to enormous size, commonly up to ten pounds.

When fresh, with slightly dingy skin and pure white flesh, puffballs are tasty and nutritious. They are usually sliced and fried in butter, but they are also good diced and added to other dishes such as soup and stew.

Coral Mushrooms

This common and widespread genus (*Clavaria*) has many similar edible species. Most of them appear in tufts or colonies and somewhat resemble heads of cauliflower.

Most of them are delicious, some are a bit tough, and a few are bitter, but none of the *Clavaria* are poisonous. One of the best is the yellow coral, which grows in enormous colonies in dense woods. It is best cooked by frying in butter after breaking the colonies into individuals.

There are a couple of general rules about mushroom picking that should be observed scrupulously, as a matter of life and death. Be absolutely sure you know the mushroom you are frying. The three varieties described above are all fairly distinctive but, except in the case of the giant puffball, it is possible to make a mistake. Buy a good guidebook and take it with you when you go prospecting for mushrooms. Learn to identify positively those mushrooms you may want to eat on backcountry trips. Bring the first few batches home to cook. If anything happens, you will at least be within reach of medical help.

Never drink alcoholic beverages while you are eating mushrooms. Alcohol can compound the effect of toxic mushrooms and can turn some innocuous varieties sour.

Many woodland mushrooms may have a slight bitter taste caused by tannic acid leached from the ground. This can be ex-

Binoculars for Birdwatching and Hunting

At left is a pair of conventional-sized 7x35 right-angle prism glasses by Bushnell.
On the right is a roof prism lightweight 8x20 by Swift that weighs just six ounces.

tracted by soaking the mushrooms in heavy brine a few hours before cooking or parboiling in salt water.

BIRDWATCHING

Among the more cheerful delights of the backcountry are the charm, diversity, and character of its birds. Species which exercise prudent timidity in built-up areas are practically gregarious in the backcountry. Others are common only to backbush areas; still other birds have retreated to the backcountry because of demanding habitat requirements or intolerance of civilization.

Like flowers, birds represent an important thread in the complicated tapestry that is the backcountry and learning about birds can give you a better understanding of the complete design. They add color and motion to the beauty of the picture.

Many of my most cherished memories of wild country feature encounters with birds. A bleak, snow-filled hanging valley high in the Mission Mountains which I shared one winter day with happy little mountain chickadees . . . bright spring days in upstate New York spent beside a seemingly barren stream listening and watching for drumming grouse . . . flights of slate-colored juncos flittering overhead as fall turned to winter in Glacier National Park . . . a dour day by a river in Scotland brightened only by the antics of a water dipper . . . or the camp-robbing gray jay who has followed me from New England through Michigan and now entertains my camps in Montana. Birds have a way of catching the eye and holding the imagination.

There are several good pocket-sized bird identification books available. Among them are the Peterson field guides to both eastern and western birds and the *Golden Field Guide to Birds of North America.*

The flora and fauna which inhabit the backcountry all play a part in our perception and appreciation of the land. If we go to all the trouble, expense, and sacrifice of journeying into these remote and often hostile places for just one purpose—hunting or fishing—we are wasting our energy and missing most of the point. The common denominator of backbush areas all over the world is their difference from the tame lands we came from. If we can't comprehend this difference, we can't appreciate the backcountry.

Index